Authors' Famous Recipes and Reflections on Food

Authors' Famous Recipes and Reflections on Food

Edited by Diane Holloway, Ph.D.

Writers Club Press
San Jose New York Lincoln Shanghai

Authors' Famous Recipes and Reflections on Food

Writers Club Press
an imprint of iUniverse, Inc.

For information address:
iUniverse, Inc.
5220 S. 16th St., Suite 200
Lincoln, NE 68512
www.iuniverse.com

ISBN: 0-595-24379-7

Printed in the United States of America

I dedicate this book to the wonderful members of the Sun Cities Authors Association who have participated in helping this to be an extraordinarily unique cookbook. These members, along with other non-members, appreciate the special talents of writers in describing everything in the world, including food. They understand the time and effort used by authors as they search to find just the right words to describe things.

"Tell me what you eat, and I will tell you what you are."
Anthelme Brillat-Savarin (1755-1826)

Contents

Preface

People who write are usually very sensitive to nuances. They take great pains to evoke reactions to their productions. They try to reach the heart of readers in every way available to them. Whether writing a poem, a book, a short story, a play, a description, a recipe, a quip, a point of view, or a feeling, they try hard to make it interesting.

There is a current trend toward including recipes in books by authors such as Nancy Pickard, Virginia Rich, Fannie Flagg, Ruth Reichl, Susan Loomis, Diane Mott Davidson, Jill Browne, Lily Prior, Frances Mayes, Laura Esquivel, and many others. They are selling well and are enjoyed by many as a way to combine reading and food. How long will they last? Will these authors be among the greats? Nobody knows but I found that this is not a new trend.

In the past, some readers have included recipes in the text of their works, such as Edmond Rostand in *Cyrano de Bergerac*, Virginia Woolf in *To the Lighthouse*, Sir Walter Scott in the Waverley novels, Mark Twain, Marjorie Kinnan Rawlings and many others.

Other writers exquisitely describe food so that it is almost possible to create recipes from their writings. This would include Willa Cather, Ernest Hemingway, O. Henry, William Thackeray, Herman Melville, George Santayana, Isak Dinesen, Jane Austen, Rex Stout, Raymond Chandler, Sir Walter Scott, and many others.

Some writers have written cookbooks in addition to other writings such as Alexander Dumas, Vincent Price, Lillian Hellman, Rex Stout, Justin Wilson, Alice B. Toklas, Thomas Jefferson, and others.

Still other writers have inspired recipes or have created recipes that have become strongly associated with them. Among these are Ian Fleming, Evelyn Waugh, Ernest Hemingway, Emile Zola, Barry Goldwater, George Simenon, John Grisham, Giacchino Rossini, Charles Dickens, Benjamin Franklin and more.

My research led me to read many recipes by writers and I came to one inescapable conclusion. Only a very few writers are able to make the directions of a recipe more interesting to read. Their talents fail them when they are simply describing "how to do it." Where they shine is in the description of the dish, their reflections on food, their ideas of what would be interesting to cook, their impressions of the role of food, and their own lives which were usually more interesting than those whose only career is to write cookbooks.

Therefore, this book is written to give a flavor of the interesting lives of those who wrote about food, and to convey some of their more astute and often humorous observations about food. But when it comes to writing the directions of the recipes, with rare exceptions, they are written the same as any other cookbook.

Acknowledgements

I wish to thank the following people for the contributions of information and for permission to use their recipes: Fae Seay, Jean Homme, Virginia Holen, Greta Manville, Phyllis Orsi, Lydia Boyer, Betty Stoneking, and Nancy Bishop.

I wish to thank Don Woolpert for his library of famous authors and to Fae Seay for suggestions of authors to be included in this book.

I am awesomely indebted to the many writers who have created and written about food over the centuries. They have shared of themselves and made their good works available to the public for enjoyment, appreciation, and consumption.

Most of all, I wish to thank my husband, historian Bob Cheney, for his advice, his reading and improvements on the manuscript, and his encouragement and support.

List of Recipes

Appetizers

Rex Stout: Bread Fried in Anchovy Butter
Diane Holloway: Catfish Pate
Lee Eyerly: Corn and Walnut Dip
Apicius: Eggs with Pignoli Sauce
Casanova: Oysters
Fae Seay: Trio Spinach Dip
Colette: Truffles

Beverages

Thomas Hardy: Ale
Ford Madox Ford: Americano
Alice B. Toklas: Blackcurrant Liqueur
Ernest Hemingway: Bloody Mary
Vincent Price: Bloody Mary
Noel Coward: Bullshot
Luis Bunuel: Bunuel Martini
Winston Churchill: Churchill Martini
Talleyrand: Coffee
Ernest Hemingway: Daiquiri
Ernest Hemingway: The Ernest Special
Ian Fleming: Fleming Martini
Raymond Chandler: Gimlet
Dashiell Hammett: Gin Gin
Somerset Maugham: Gin Pahit

Salads

Black Turkey

Vegetables and Side Dishes

Breads and Rolls

Mark Twain: Ash Cake
William Oliver: Bath Buns
Vincent Price: Bread
Marjorie K. Rawlings: Cornbread
Rex Stout: Corn Pancakes with Sauce
Tennessee Williams: Croissants
Sir Walter Scott: Diet Loaf
Justin Wilson: Hush Puppies
Thomas Jefferson: Monticello Muffins
Apicius: Pancakes With Milk
Sir Walter Scott: Parlies
Sophie Burden: Remuda Dude Ranch Beer Biscuits

Desserts

Edmond Rostand: Almond Tartlets
Dr. Ruth: Almost As Good As Sex Cheesecake
Alexander Dumas: Apricot Compote
Isak Dinesen: Baba au Rhum
Emily Dickinson: Black Cake
Thomas Jefferson: Blancmange with Brandied Apricots
Vincent Price: Boccone Dolce
Marie Antoinette: Cake
James Thurber: Devil's Food Cake
Daniel Bowen: Damper
Baghdad, 8th century: Dates in Saffron
Abigail Van Buren: Dear Abby's Pecan Pie
Vincent Price: Gingerbread
Thomas Jefferson: Ice Cream
Sigmund Freud: Incredible Oedipal Pie
Edith Buxbaum: Kaiserschmarrn

Cookies and Candy

Chapter 1

APPETIZERS

Recipe for a Hippopotamus Sandwich

A hippo sandwich is easy to make.
All you do is simply take
One slice of bread,
One slice of cake,
Some mayonnaise
One onion ring,
One hippopotamus
One piece of string,
A dash of pepper
That ought to do it.
And now comes the problem...
Biting into it.
Shel Silverstein (1930-1999)

"Butter of the most unimpeachable freshness." Mark Twain (1835-1910)

Bread Fried in Anchovy Butter

Rex Stout (1896-1975) grew up as a Quaker. After graduating from high school in Topeka, Kansas, he attended the University of Kansas. This recipe was mentioned in his mystery novel, *The Mother Hunt* published in 1963. It featured obese sleuth Nero Wolfe, who weighed in at one-seventh of a ton or 286 pounds. One of Wolfe's epicurean delights in this book was bread triangles fried in anchovy butter. The recipe appeared in Stout's *Nero Wolfe Cookbook*, and it is available on the Internet.

Anchovy Butter:
- 8 anchovy fillets
- Juice of 1 lemon or 1 ounce of cognac
- 1 tablespoon fresh parsley, chopped
- 1 cup sweet softened butter

Mash the anchovy fillets with the juice or cognac until all the juice has been incorporated. Mix in the parsley. Add the mixture to the butter and beat well to form a smooth paste. Pack into a small crock and refrigerate for at least one hour before using.

Bread Fried in Anchovy Butter:
- 12 pieces white bread
- ½ cup anchovy butter

Trim the crusts from the bread and cut the slices into triangles. Butter one side of each slice with anchovy butter and set aside. Heat two tablespoons of the butter in a large skillet and arrange as many triangles in the pan as possible. When they are golden brown on the bottom, turn and cook them on the other side. Add more butter as needed. Serve warm. Serves 4.

"Down in the meadow by a little bitty pool
Swam three little fishies and the mama fishie too.
'Swim', said the mama fishie, 'swim if you can',
And they swam and they swam all over the dam."
Saxie Dowell

Catfish Pate

Dr. Diane Holloway, psychologist and author from Dallas, Texas, co-authored *Before You Say 'I Quit'* with Nancy Bishop and wrote *The Mind of Oswald, Dallas and the Jack Ruby Trial, American History in Song,* and *Analyzing Leaders, Presidents and Terrorists.*

Many claim that catfish is not a noble fish, but this elegant appetizer puts such rumors to the test. People from the South know that the delicate flavor of the catfish lends itself to the ingredients with which it is cooked, and its texture is quite succulent.

- 1 pound catfish fillets
- ½ cup water
- ½ cup vermouth
- 16 ounces cream cheese
- 1 clove garlic, minced
- 2 tablespoons fresh lemon juice
- 2 teaspoons Creole seasoning
- 1 teaspoon liquid smoke

- 1/8 teaspoon pepper to taste
- ¼ cup parsley, chopped

Poach the catfish in water and vermouth until it flakes with a fork. Drain and combine fish with other ingredients except parsley. Mash to form a ball and chill. Cover the ball with chopped parsley before serving. Serve with crackers, chips or garlic toast rounds. Makes 16 servings.

"The corn is as high as an elephant's eye,
An' it looks like it's climbing clear up to the sky."
Oscar Hammerstein, II (1895-1960)

Corn and Walnut Dip

This recipe came from the Flying E Ranch, one of the original "dude ranches" in Wickenburg, Arizona. Wickenburg was called the "Dude Ranch Capital of the World" and attracted people from the turn of the century until the present, with its heyday during the 1920s and 1930s.

Colorful writer and pilot, Lee Eyerly, owned the Flying E. Eyerly founded the Eyerly Aircraft Company, was an inventor and created various amusement rides such as the Loop-O-Plane, Roll-O-Plane, Rock-O-Plane, Spider, and others. His writings reveal many plans and inventions, which he patented, but never actually developed.

The ranch is still operated by owner Vi Wellik and this Mexican dip is still used to welcome guests for chuck wagon dinners.

- 2 eight ounce packages cream cheese, soft
- ¼ cup vegetable oil
- ¼ cup lime juice

- 1 tablespoon ground red chilies
- 1 tablespoon ground cumin
- ½ teaspoon salt
- Dash pepper
- 1 can (8 ¾ oz.) drained whole kernel corn
- 1 cup chopped walnuts
- ¼ cup chopped green onion

Beat the first seven ingredients in a large bowl on medium setting on eggbeater until smooth. Stir in corn, walnuts and onion. Makes four cups of dip. Serve with tortilla chips.

"Put all your eggs in the one basket and watch that basket!" Mark Twain (1835-1910)

Eggs with Pignoli Sauce

Marcus Gavius Apicius de re Coquinaria (1st century) wrote the oldest cookbook in existence. He taught haute cuisine to the staff of the Roman emperors. It is said that fearing he would not be able to eat fine food in his old age, he committed suicide.

In actuality, there were three Apicius chefs and it not absolutely known which one of them wrote the cookbook. This is one of the strange and interesting recipes from the cookbook.

There were several elements and levels in Apicius' cooking. First were the sauces in which he combined crushed green herbs (lovage, oregano, thyme) with ground spices such as pepper, cumin and coriander. The second level was to make food sweet with honey or sour with vinegar. The third level was to combine raisins, dates and plums with almonds, walnuts and chestnuts. The fourth level was to cook foods in either wine or stock.

- 2 ounces pine nuts (pignoli)
- 3 tablespoons red wine vinegar
- 1 teaspoon honey
- A pinch of pepper
- A pinch of celery leaf
- 4 eggs (boiled four minutes)

Place the pine nuts in the vinegar to linger for four hours. Make a puree with the honey, pepper and celery leaf in a blender. Slice the eggs and allow guests to add as much sauce to the eggs as they wish, according to their palette. You may keep the sauce for days.

Serve with mead, a honeyed wine. Make it by adding half a cup of heated clear honey to a bottle of white wine. Stir and chill. Romans had only cool cellars so chill only to about 50 degrees.

"The oyster's a confusing suitor
It's masc., and fem., and even neuter.
But whether husband, pal or wife
It leads a painless sort of life.
I'd like to be an oyster, say,
In August, June, July or May."
Ogden Nash (1902-1971)

Oysters

Giovanni Casanova de Seingalt (1725-1798) is known for his autobiography called *Memoirs*. He was a remarkable man who lived a risky life searching for pleasure, passion and brave feats to perform. His appetizer before the evening meal was often a dozen oysters. This was probably to prepare for late night amours since oysters were thought to be an aphrodisiac. He would have eaten them either raw or cooked (usually in wine).

Raw oysters that were not kept cold enough could lead to stomach upsets and worse, thus it became popular to eat them only in months with an "R" in their name, all of which are cold months. This version of raw oysters popular during Casanova's time might have been to his liking.

- 12 oysters in the shell
- Kosher salt
- 1 shallot, finely minced
- Freshly ground pepper
- ¼ cup or more dry white wine
- 1 lemon cut in wedges
- Oyster knife required

Put kosher salt on two chilled plates. Carefully balance 6 oysters per person on each plate. Mix together the shallot, wine and pepper and spoon a little over each oyster. Garnish with the lemon wedges. To eat, use the oyster shells as spoons and drink the liquor along with the oysters. Oysters should be enjoyed with a glass of very cold white wine such as Champagne, Chardonnay, Sauvignon Blanc or Chablis.

Shucking Oysters: To shuck fresh oysters you will need an oyster knife. Work over a bowl to catch any oyster juices. Protecting your hand with a thick kitchen towel, grip an oyster, flat side up. With the tip of the oyster knife, pry around the hinge to open. Run the knife along the flat side to loosen the oyster, and then carefully loosen the oyster on the cupped side of the shell. Discard any loose bits of shell.

"What a world of gammon and spinach it is, though, ain't it?" Charles Dickens (1812-1870)

Trio Spinach Dip

Fae Seay collected this recipe from a Little Rock, Arkansas, restaurant called Trio's. The Cavender's Greek Seasoning, made in Harrison, Arkansas, is available most places. Spinach dishes were favorites of writers like Evelyn Waugh, Justin Wilson, Robert Graves, and Rex Stout.

- 1 8 ounce package cream cheese
- 1 can mild Rotel, drained
- 1 12 ounce package shredded cheese, Mexican mix
- 1 small onion, chopped
- 1 clove garlic, minced
- 1 package frozen spinach, uncooked, thawed, with all water removed

Mix all and bake 20-30 minutes at 350 degrees. Best if served warm. Serve with pita chips, buttered, cut, and sprinkled with Cavender's Greek seasoning.

"Even a blind hog can find an acorn now and then," was a quotation from Friedrich Nietzsche but it was often combined with a mental image of a pig rooting for truffles in the forest sniffing truffles buried at the base of oak trees.

Truffles

Colette (Sidonie Gabrielle), a French novelist (1873-1954) is most known for her novel *Gigi*. She was said to have discovered the unknown actress (Audrey Hepburn) to play the leading role in the movie of the same name. She reported on the Italian front in World War I and wrote a column in the Parisian newspaper, *Le Matin*. This recipe for the esteemed mushroom called truffles gives an example of her wit and culinary expertise, and it is available on the Internet.

"Steep in good very dry white wine. Keep your champagne for banquets; the truffle (highly prized black or white mushroom sniffed out by pigs and dogs) does very well without it. Lightly seasoned with salt and pepper. Cook in a covered black cocotte (black iron skillet). For 25 minutes it dances in the boiling liquid … which give substance to the cooking juices. No other spices whatsoever! To hell with the pressed napkin, tasting and smelling of chlorine, the final bed of the cooked truffle. Your truffles should come to the table in their court-bouillon (cooking liquid.) Take a generous helping: the truffle whets the appetite and assists the digestion."

Chapter 2

BEVERAGES

Ale: Inspiration for Fancies

Filled with mingled cream and amber
I will drain that glass again.
Such hilarious visions clamber
Through the chambers of my brain
Quaintest thoughts, queerest fancies
Come to life and fade away;
Who cares how time advances?
I am drinking ale today.
Edgar Allen Poe (1809-1849)

"Why does man kill? He kills for food. And not only food; frequently there must be a beverage." Woody Allen

Ale

Thomas Hardy (1840-1928) wrote such books as *Tess of the D'Ubervilles, The Return of the Native* and *Mayor of Casterbridge.* In the latter, he wrote with enthusiasm about the ale of Casterbridge in Dorchester, England. As a result, the Eldridge Pope Brewery named their ale after him in 1968. Thomas Hardy Ale is available in some distribution centers in the United States as well and has a distinctive pineapple hint. While it is rare to find those interested in making ale, this close version of the ale with a similar aroma can be made by those with the right equipment, and it is available on the Internet.

- 15 pounds pale-ale malt (M & F from England)
- 2 pounds light brown sugar

Hops: Chinook for boil, circa 25 HBU
Fuggles for finish, circa 1 ounce 2 mins.
Chinook 1/8 dry hop
Fuggles ¼ dry hop
Mash: 15 quarts water
Mash in 130, raise to 158 F. Hold for 1 ½ hours
Sparge with 30 quarts at 170 F. Add 1 teaspoon gypsum.
Boil about 6 hours. Add bittering hops 60 minutes before the end of boil.
Wort should be 3.5-4 gallons gravity, gravity 1.30-1.145
Yeast: 1028 w yeast
After 7 days, rack into 5 gallon carbouy and pitch champagne yeast.
Let ferment 4-6 days, then rack into 30 gallon carbouy.

If you don't have one, flush a 5 gallon with dry ice to remove oxygen.
Dry hop with hop bag for 2 weeks.
Remove hop bag, let sit an additional month.
Bottle: There may be little carbonation. Add some champagne yeast when bottling. Use corn sugar to prime: About 1/3 cup.

"If your doctor does not think it good for you to sleep, to drink wine, or to eat of a particular dish, do not worry; I will find you another who will not agree with him. Michel de Montaigne (1533-1592)

Americano

Ford Madox Ford was a writer, painter and promoter of other literary figures such as Joseph Conrad. He wrote *The Good Soldier, Parade's End*, created the *"transatlantic review"* and painted *Maundy Thursday,* and hung around with the literati in Paris during the 1920s and 1930s in Gertrude Stein and Alice Toklas's salon. He especially liked sweet red vermouth, hence this recipe.

- 1 part Campari
- 1 part red vermouth
- Ice
- Lemon slice
- Soda water, if desired for carbonation

Mix all and drink.

"Quickly, bring me a beaker of wine, so that I may wet my mind and say something clever." Aristophanes (448-385 B.C.)

Blackcurrant Liqueur

Alice B. Toklas (1877-1967) wrote a cookbook that was published in 1954. She was the lover and publisher for Gertrude Stein who died in 1946. The two were important mainstays in the literary scene in Paris during the 1920s and 1930s. Toklas was fascinated by many dishes from France and Spain and besides creating her own versions of recipes, she published authentic local recipes and recipes of other literati friends.

This is a modest version of her recipe for black currant liqueur, which is also known as cassis, and it is available on the Internet.

- ½ cup raspberries
- 3 cups black currants
- 1 tablespoon black currant leaves
- ½ cup vodka
- 3 cups sugar
- ¼ cup water

Wash and drain fruit and put in a plastic or glass bowl. Crush thoroughly. Cover with a cheesecloth to sit for 24 hours. Then add leaves and vodka. Cover and allow to sit for another 24 hours. Then pour through a sieve into other bowl. Boil the sugar and water for 5 minutes stirring often. Remove and cool the syrup. Add syrup to fruit and allow to sit for several hours. Filter through a cheesecloth into a bottle. The liqueur may be served immediately or aged a few days or weeks.

"Drink not the third glass which thou canst not tame,
When once it is within thee."
George Herbert (1563-1633)

Bloody Mary

Ernest Hemingway (1899-1961) wrote very specific directions in a letter to a friend about how to make a Bloody Mary. Hemingway lived a hard life with travels to many countries, four wives, heavy drinking, and risky endeavors. He finally committed suicide in Ketcham, Idaho, when his health and his creditors were taking their toll. This recipe is available on the Internet and gives an idea of why his life did not last longer. The spelling errors were his emphasis.

- Russian vodka
- Chilled tomato juice
- 1 tablespoon Worcestershire Sauce
- Juice of 1 lime
- Celery salt
- Cayenne pepper
- Black pepper

"To make a pitcher of Blood Marys (any smaller amount is worthless) take a good sized pitcher and put in it as big a lump of ice as it will hold. (This is to prevent too rapid melting and watering of our product.) Mix a pint of good Russian vodka and an equal amount of chilled tomato juice. Add a tablespoonful of Worcestershire Sauce. Lea and Perrin is usual but can use A 1 or any good beef steak sauce. Stirr. Then add a jigger of fresh squeezed lime juice. Stirr. Then add small amounts of celery salt, cayenne pepper, black pepper.

"Keep on stirring and taste it to see how it is doing. If you get it too powerful weaken with more tomato juice. If it lacks authority add more vodka. Some people like more lime than others. For combating a really terrific hangover increase the amount of Worcestershire Sauce but don't lose the lovely color.

"Keep drinking it yourself to see how it is doing. After you get the hang of it you can mix it so it will taste as though it had absolutely no alcohol of any kind in it and a glass of it will still have as much kick as a really good big martini. Whole trick is to keep it very cold and not let the ice water it down. Use good vodka and good tomato juice.

"There is a very fine Mexican sauce called Esta Si Pican (sort of mild tabasco) that is good added to the Bloody Marys, too. Just a few drops."

"You can't eat for eight hours a day, nor drink for eight hours, nor make love for eight hours a day; all you can do for eight hours a day is work." William Faulkner (1897-1962)

Bloody Mary

Who should know more about a Bloody Mary than Vincent Price (1911-1993) who played in many horror films? In addition, Price was a connoisseur of art with a bachelors and masters degree in art. His father directed a national candy company in St. Louis, Missouri, and he grew up in a cultured home with fine food.

Vincent and his second wife, Mary, wrote *A Treasury of Great Recipes in 1965*. Compare this version of Bloody Mary with others and you will find it hot, sweet and sour at the same time and, as Vincent said, these Bloody Marys "show their fist." This recipe is available on the Internet.

- 6 jiggers vodka
- 6 drops Tabasco
- 6 dashes Worcestershire sauce
- 6 tablespoons lime juice
- ½ teaspoon salt
- 1 teaspoon freshly ground pepper
- 2 teaspoons sugar
- ¼ teaspoon MSG (optional)
- 2 medium cans V-8 juice

In a large pitcher, mix vodka, Tabasco, Worcestershire, lime juice, salt, pepper, MSG, sugar, and V-8. Stir well and pour into glasses over ice.

"Mad dogs and Englishmen go out in the midday sun." Noel Coward

Bullshot

Noel Coward (1899-1973) was an Englishman who wrote poems, short stories, plays, songs, novels, and acted in plays, musicals, and movies. Some works he wrote were made into movies such as *Private Lives, Cavalcade, Design for Living, Blithe Spirit, In Which We Serve* and *Brief Encounter.* Some of his songs were *Mad About the Boy, Someone to Watch Over Me, Let's Say Goodbye, I've Been to a Marvelous Party, Time and Again, Mad Dogs and Englishmen,* and *Do Do Do.*

Noel's favorite drink was the Bullshot which he enjoyed many places in the world including Raffles Hotel in Singapore.

- 2-3 ice cubes
- 1 ½ or 2 ounces gin
- 3 ounces chilled beef bouillon

Put ice cubes in an Old fashioned glass. Add gin and bouillon and stir gently. Alternatively, vodka may be used instead of gin. Serves 1.

"Connoisseurs who like their martinis very dry suggest simply allowing a ray of sunlight to shine through a bottle of Noilly Prat before it hits the bottle of gin." Luis Bunuel (1900-1983)

Bunuel Martini

Luis Bunuel (1900-1983), the late Spanish surrealist director of movies, wrote much dialogue for his award winning films. He also loved martinis and believed them to be a classic American invention.

Among his movies were *Un Chien Andalou, L'Age D'Or, Los Olvidados, The Exterminating Angel, Simon of the Desert, The Criminal Life of Archibaldo de la Cruz, Nazarine, The Discreet Charm of the Bourgeoisie,* and others. He was able to get his version of a martini in the latter film, which won a 1972 Academy Award for the best foreign language film. This recipe is available on the Internet.

- Chill glasses, gin and shaker the day before
- Fill shaker with ice
- A few drops of Noilly Prat vermouth
- Add a half demitasse spoon of Angostura Bitters
- Shake, pour out liquids leaving only ice

- Gin
- Olive

The ice retains the vermouth and bitters taste so add gin just to the ice, shake and pour into a glass. Add an olive.

Lady Astor told Churchill, "Sir, if you were my husband, I would poison your drink." He replied, "Madam, if you were my wife, I would drink it."

Churchill Martini

Winston Churchill (1871-1947) began his career as a war correspondent covering the Boer War in South Africa. He was captured and escaped dramatically becoming an instant hero. He continued to write and became more involved in legislation of the welfare state, then lord of the admiralty, and led a naval campaign.

He wrote the 5-volume edition of *The World Crisis* after he lost his seat in Parliament. He was brought back into government as Prime Minister of England and inspired resistance to Nazi Germany during World War II. He also wrote *The History of the English Speaking Peoples* and a series called *The Second World War.* He received the Nobel Prize in Literature in 1953.

He, like all Prime Ministers of England, had to contend with neighboring French leaders, who demanded respect and inclusion in plans. Churchill enjoyed martinis and had his own interesting version reflecting Anglo-French diplomacy. This description is available on the Internet.

- 3 ounces London dry gin
- Lemon peel to garnish

Stir gin in a cocktail shaker with ice until very cold. Turn toward the direction of France and bow before straining into a chilled shallow glass. Add garnish.

"Making coffee has become the great compromise of the decade. It's the only thing 'real men' do that doesn't seem to threaten their masculinity." Erma Bombeck (1927-1996)

Coffee

Charles Maurice de Talleyrand-Perigord (1754-1838) wrote this poetic recipe for coffee. Talleyrand was the most important French diplomat in their history, and served his country during the French Revolution and afterwards by traveling about Europe and negotiating with heads of state. He was Napoleon's trusted ally until later years. His visits to America caused him to write essays describing the importance the colonies could have for France. He was a bon vivant and lover of women, and judging by this poem, loved coffee avidly as well.

"Black as the devil,
Hot as hell,
Pure as an angel,
Sweet as love."

"Bad men live that they may eat and drink whereas good men eat and drink that they may live." Socrates (469-399 B.C.)

Daiquiri

Many attest to Ernest Hemingway's (1899-1961) love for a late afternoon mouth-puckering cold Daiquiri. He never had a frozen daiquiri, which had not yet been invented. When he prepared this drink, he always included these three ingredients. This description is available on the Internet.

Hemingway and many other writers drank to excess, shortening their lives and wrecking relationships. The use of alcohol by writers appears exceptionally high and may have something to do with the lonely business of writing. However, there are equally good writers who had no problem with overindulgence so there is an unlikely connection between creativity and alcohol.

It was after drinking daiquiris that he had a car wreck in the 1950s. He married his fourth wife, Mary, who helped care for him despite numerous affairs he continued to have. They lived in Finca, Cuba, and he proclaimed support for Fidel Castro and the revolutionaries in 1959. In poor health, he left Cuba in 1960 and was treated for alcoholism and depression in Idaho before he killed himself as his father had done, with a gunshot wound to the head.

- Rum
- Granulated sugar
- Fresh lime juice

Mix in a shaker with crushed ice, using the proportions you desire.

"I need an hour alone before dinner, with a drink, to go over what I've done that day. I can't do it in the afternoon because I'm too close to it. Also the drink helps. It removes me from the pages. So I spend this hour taking things out and putting other things in." Joan Didion

The Ernest Special

Ernest Hemingway (1899-1961) introduced this drink to Peter Buckley in Spain. It was probably created during Hemingway's time in Cuba. This description is available on the Internet. Hemingway, whose father was a pediatrician, needed to demonstrate his masculinity. This search to believe that he was not soft was apparent in his drinking, love life, safaris, bull fighting, and love of guns.

Having been raised by very religious parents, Ernest was constantly suffering from guilt whenever he displeased his parents, his wives, or his children. His tortured soul received some apparent respite when he drank.

- 1 generous shot of Scotch
- 1 generous shot of fresh lime juice

Pour Scotch and lime juice into a tumbler over ice. Serve.

"I never had more than one drink before dinner. But I do like that one to be large and very strong and very cold and very well-made," said James Bond in *Casino Royale* by Ian Fleming.

Fleming Martini

Early in life, Ian Fleming was overshadowed by the success and wealth of his grandfather, father and brother. As an aside, reporter Winston Churchill wrote his father's obituary for an English newspaper.

After an indifferent attempt at universities, he moved to Austria where he began to develop his own distinctive life. He became a reporter, a banker, and then an intelligence agent with espionage expertise. After brilliant success he helped "Wild Bill" Donovan start the OSS in the U.S., the early version of the CIA.

Fleming eventually established a life split between Jamaica and the continent. He had his first success with *Casino Royale* and a character named James Bond. Fleming was a hard drinker himself, as was his character.

He had two versions of martinis in his James Bond novels. In *Casino Royale*, Bond drank this martini. This recipe is available on the Internet.

- 3 measures of Gordon's gin
- 1 measure of vodka
- ½ measure of Kina Lillet vermouth
- Lemon peel garnish

Shake until ice cold. Pour in champagne glass. Garnish with lemon peel.

In other novels, James Bond drank this vodka martini.

- 2 parts vodka (preferably Russian)
- 1 part dry vermouth
- Twist of lemon rind

Place four or five ice cubes in a cocktail shaker, add the vodka and vermouth and shake well. Strain the mixture into a cocktail glass and decorate it with a twist of lemon rind.

"Hey! Who took the cork off my lunch?" W. C. Fields (1880-1946)

Gimlet

Raymond Chandler (1888-1959) wrote many mysteries and movie screenplays including *Double Indemnity, Strangers on a Train, The Blue Dahlia, The Big Sleep, Farewell My Lovely,* etc. He created a mystery series with private eye Philip Marlow, who set a new tone in American novels as a detective with a strong code of ethics.

Chandler was born in the United States but lived in England with his mother after her divorce. He was educated in England and later studied international law in France and Germany. He became a substitute teacher in an English college preparatory school and wrote poetry and short stories early.

He returned to America in 1912 where he worked on a ranch, in a sporting goods store, was a bookkeeper, and then joined the Canadian Army in World War I. He was transferred to the RAF and soon after the war, married a divorcee 18 years older than he. He became a banker but studied Erle Stanley Gardner's style and wrote his first full novel in 1933. After it sold, his wife told him to stop working and spend his time writing.

In *The Long Goodbye*, Marlowe's troubled war buddy, Terry Lennox, described a Gimlet. It apparently became Marlowe's favorite drink because it appeared in many novels, but his addition of bitters depended upon circumstances. Others say that the ideal proportion for a Gimlet is 3 parts gin to 1 part Rose's Lime Juice. Chandler even had Marlowe discuss the virtues of making a Gimlet with vodka instead of gin but here was their basic dialogue.

"What they call a Gimlet is just some lime or lemon juice and gin with a dash of sugar and bitters," Lennox says while ensconced in a Los Angeles bar. "A real gimlet is half gin and half Rose's Lime Juice and nothing else. It beats martinis hollow."

"I drove out to Victor's with the idea of drinking a Gimlet and sitting around until the evening edition of the morning papers was on the street. But the bar was crowded and it wasn't any fun. When the barkeep I knew got around to me he called me by name. 'You like a dash of bitters in it, don't you?' 'Not usually. Just for tonight, two dashes of bitters.'" Marlow had just finished the case and was celebrating.

- 1 part gin
- 1 part Rose's Lime Juice
- Optional: Dash of Angostura Bitters
- Ice

Mix, shake and drink.

"Oh, it's beer if you're bent on expansion,
And wine if you wish to grow thin,
But quaffers who think of a drink as a drink,
When they quaff, quaff of whisky and gin."
Ogden Nash (1902-1971)

Gin Gin

Dashiell Hammett developed a private eye named Sam Spade who appeared in some of his books like *The Maltese Falcon*. Hammett had worked for the Pinkerton Detective Agency before World War I, but when called into the military contracted tuberculosis and spent the rest of the war in hospital. Afterwards, he wrote copy for a jewelry store until he fell upon some success as a writer.

In the 1930s, he joined the Communist Party. In 1951, he went to prison for five months rather than testify against others at the McCarthy hearings. He taught writing in New York toward the end of his life, and was cared for by Lillian Hellman until he died of lung cancer, penniless.

Hellman was enjoying her own success as a writer for such stories as *Watch On the Rhine.* When she and Hammett began their relationship, he wrote the *Thin Man* mystery series about Nick and Nora Charles and the cocktail set. Nick, a former detective, married a rich woman, Nora, who was based on Lillian Hellman. Hammett also wrote many short stories, often describing drinks. In "The Big Knockover," he described a drink composed of gin and ginger ale.

"In the middle of the floor one of Larrouy's girls began to sing 'Tell Me What You Want and I'll Tell You What You Get.' Paddy the Mex tipped a gin bottle over the glasses of ginger ale the waiter had brought."

"She (Sadie Thompson) gathered herself together. No one could describe the scorn of her expression or the contemptuous hatred she put into her answer. "You men! You filthy dirty pigs! You're all the same, all of you. Pigs! Pigs!"
Somerset Maugham

Gin Pahit

Somerset Maugham (1874-1965) wrote *Of Human Bondage, Cakes and Ale, The Moon and Sixpence, Liza of Lambeth, The Summing Up* and numerous short stories such as *Rain.* He used to write about rubber plantation owners of Malaysia who stayed at Raffles Hotel. In some stories, they are being served Gin Pahits by servants. Raffles Hotel opened in Singapore in 1887 and served the wealthy including writers Joseph Conrad, Noel Coward and others.

- 1.5 ounces gin
- .5 ounce Angostura bitters
- Ice
- Optional: lemon juice or sugar

Shake ingredients well and strain into a cold glass.

"I exercise extreme self control. I never have anything stronger than gin before breakfast." W. C. Fields (1880-1946)

Hemingway Martini

Ernest Hemingway used to frequent Harry's Bar in Venice. The house specialty was the Montgomery Martini named for the WWII British general. Harry's Bar was a place he enjoyed for the atmosphere as much as the drinks. It was opened in 1928 and had specialties of cocktails and sandwiches but has now expanded to offer exquisite dining.

Hemingway also enjoyed the restrooms of many of his favorite bars and claimed to want the urinal of Harry's Bar if it was ever to be sold. This recipe for the Montgomery Martini was available on the Internet.

- 3 ounces Gordon's gin
- 1 teaspoon plus a few drops of Noilly Prat vermouth
- Olive

Pour the gin and vermouth in a shaker with ice. Shake. Pour into glasses to be kept in the freezer for a few minutes until ready to serve. Garnish with an olive.

"I must get out of these wet clothes and into a dry martini." Robert Benchley (1889-1945)

Hitchcock Martini

Alfred Hitchcock (1889-1980) was not only a great director but wrote many of the lines for his famous movies. Raised as a Jesuit Catholic, he attended college learning engineering, navigation, and art. He began his career by creating captions for silent movies. He learned scripting, editing, art direction and rose to assistant director of movies by the time talking movies emerged.

His film direction included emphasis on dialogue, suspense, surprise and shock. He married an assistant screenwriter to whom he remained married until his death in 1980. His most outstanding films were *The Lodger, The Man Who Knew Too Much, 39 Steps, Suspicion, Rebecca, Shadow of a Doubt, Notorious, Strangers on a Train, I Confess, Dial M for Murder, To Catch a Thief, Rear Window, Vertigo, North by Northwest, Psycho* and *The Birds.*

His martini recipe displayed his British humor and his love of gin. This recipe and description is available on the Internet.

- 5 ounces London dry gin
- Lemon peel garnish

Stir gin in a cocktail shaker with ice until very cold. Tap a bottle of extra dry vermouth against the shaker three times. Strain into a well-chilled glass and garnish with lemon peel.

"Did you ever taste beer?"
"I had a sip of it once," said the small servant.
"Here's a state of things!" cried Mr. Swiveller..."She never tasted it; it can't be tasted in a sip!" Charles Dickens

Hot Punch

Charles Dickens (1812-1870) wrote *Bleak House, A Christmas Carol, David Copperfield, Great Expectations, Hard Times, The Mystery of Edwin Drood, Nicholas Nickleby, The Old Curiosity Shop, Oliver Twist, Pickwick Papers, A Tale of Two Cities,* and many other works.

This recipe came from a letter that Charles Dickens wrote in 1847. The recipe was published in *The Charles Dickens Cookbook* by Brenda Marshall. This is a very strong punch and should be served in small quantities.

- Zest of lemons, cut into several pieces each
- 1 cup brown sugar, packed
- 2 cups dark rum
- ½ cup brandy
- Juice of 3 lemons
- 4 cups very hot water
- More sugar to taste
- Optional: cinnamon sticks

In a 4 quart saucepan combine the lemon zest, sugar, rum and brandy. Warm over low heat. Be sure there's no exhaust fan running. Stand well back as you light the liquid with a long match. When the flames have gone out, stir in the lemon juice and the water. Taste for sugar.

Bring the punch to a very gentle bubble, cover completely and cook 10 minutes. Remove the lemon zest.

Set aside up to 3 hours, or refrigerate overnight. Serve warm, ladled into cups with handles.

"The wine urges me on, the bewitching wine, which sets even a wise man to singing and to laughing gently and rouses him up to dance and brings forth words which were better unspoken." Homer, from *The Iliad*

Liberace

Lawrence Sanders (1920-1998), created the wonderful mystery novels featuring Detective Edward X. Delaney. He was born in Brooklyn and spent his first 20 years of writing in journalism. He burst onto the literary scene in 1970 with *The Anderson Tapes* which introduced Delaney. He also created the Commandment Series and the Sin Series with works like *The First Deadly Sin* and *The Sixth Commandment*.

He also has been accused of creating the Liberace after the famous entertainer wowed television audiences by playing dazzling pieces on a piano with a candelabra. This unusual drink "lights up" the table.

- 1/3 part Kahlua or Tia Maria
- 1/3 part milk or cream
- 1/3 part rum

Pour the liqueur into a thick glass. Carefully layer the milk or cream on top of it. Then carefully pour the rum on top. Light the rum. After it burns a few seconds, blow it out and drink it. This should be the first drink of the evening because you don't want to spill the rum and start a fire on you, your friends, or the house.

"There is something they put in a highball
That awakens the torpidest brain,
That kindles a spark in the eyeball,
Gliding, singing through vein after vein.
There is something they put in a highball
Which you'll notice one day, if you watch;
And it may be the soda, but judged by the odor,
I rather believe it's the Scotch."
Ogden Nash (1902-1971)

Mailer Martini

Norman Mailer was born in New Jersey and raised in Brooklyn. He was married six times and has nine children. At the age of 9, he wrote a 250 page story called *Invasion From Mars*. He attended Harvard and after serving in the Army in WWII, enrolled in the Sorbonne in Paris.

His first major work was *The Naked and the Dead* when he was 25. It was about his experiences in the war in the Philippines. He became a Hollywood script writer and had uncertain success for some years. In 1960, he stabbed his artist wife (Adele) and was given a suspended sentence. He once described himself as a "white Negro."

He wanted to advise President Kennedy and wrote *The Presidential Papers* in 1963. Later he wrote the biography of Marilyn Monroe, wrote about Lee Harvey Oswald and believed him to be the lone assassin of President Kennedy

He also wrote *Harlot's Ghost* and had a CIA Station Chief in West Berlin call his martini "smooth fire, sweet ice." Here was his recipe which is also available on the Internet.

- 2 ounces Bombay Sapphire gin
- ½ ounce single malt scotch
- Lemon peel garnish

Fill a shaker with ice. Rub lemon peel around the bottom of the martini glass. Shake martini, strain and pour into the glass.

"It's funny how you get a run," he said. "Take last night. There was at least ten guys ordered Manhattans. Sometimes you don't get two calls for a Manhattan in a month. It's the grenadine give the stuff that taste." John Steinbeck (1902-1968)

Manhattan

Vincent Price was well known as an actor, chef, and author of *A Treasury of Great Recipes.* He was even prouder of his book *The Vincent Price Treasury of American Art.* He was also the spokesman for certain food products including Angostura bitters, which he particularly favored in drinks and food. Some used grenadine in their Manhattans but not Price. This recipe was available on the Internet on an ad for Angostura Bitters.

- 2/3 parts good whiskey
- 1/3 part sweet vermouth
- 2 dashes Angostura

Mix with ice. "Stupendous," said Vincent.

"Eat not to dullness; drink not to elevation." Benjamin Franklin

Milk Punch

Benjamin Franklin (1706-1790) was unable to pursue schooling for the ministry because his family was too poor. He began to work in print shops and eventually founded the *Pennsylvania Gazette* in which he wrote various anonymous letters and articles.

Besides participating in the creation of many documents in the formation of the United States government, he also wrote homilies in addition to agricultural and astronomical data in *Poor Richard's Almanack*.

He created the *American Philosophical Society,* reorganized the fire department, started a movement to pave and light the streets, and established an academy which later became the University of Pennsylvania. He invented an improved form of heating stove, established a militia, and experimented with lightning power.

He later wrote his famous autobiography first published under the title of *Memoires* in Paris, and republished in America as *The Autobiography of Benjamin Franklin.* It was done in the form of letters to his son.

This recipe was contained in a letter to James Bowodin on October 11, 1763, and is in the Massachusetts Historical Society.

- 6 quarts of brandy
- Rinds of 44 lemon pared very thin

- 4 large nutmegs, grated
- 2 quarts of lemon juice
- 2 pounds of refined sugar
- 4 quarts of water
- 3 quarts of milk

Steep the rinds in the brandy 24 hours, then strain it off. Combine the water, lemon juice, sugar and nutmeg. When the sugar is dissolved, boil the milk and add to the brandy and sugar water mixture. Stir it about and let stand two hours. Pass through a jelly bag and bottle.

This makes enough for about 120 servings of 4 ounces each. Franklin must have had some very big parties or some guests who may drink to elevation, contradicting the Franklin quotation above.

"There is something about a mint julep.
It is nectar imbibed in a dream,
As fresh as the bud of the tulip,
As cool as the bed of the stream.
There is something about a mint julep,
A fragrance beloved by the lucky.
And perhaps it's the tint of the frost and the mint,
But I think it was born in Kentucky."
Ogden Nash (1902-1971)

Mint Julep

Daniel Rogov, wine critic for an Israeli daily newspaper and wine consultant to Hugh Johnson's *Pocket Encyclopedia of Wine*, has the perfect Mint Julep recipe. This description was available on the Internet under

Rogov's column entitled *Rogov's Ramblings*. William Faulkner (1897-1962) who is being discussed in this article is known for having said, "The tools I need for my work are paper, tobacco, food and a little whiskey."

"The image, at least according to William Faulkner, is complete only if the table is set in the middle of an unimaginably large, perfectly green lawn… The men will be wearing suits and ties and the women will be wearing long dresses, unspeakably high-heeled shoes and large flowered hats.

"To make a perfect mint julep, place 1 ½ teaspoons of confectioner's sugar and 5 or 6 sprigs of mint in a tall glass that has a capacity of between 225 and 250 milliliters. Add 1 tablespoon of cold water and with a wooden spoon, mix well making sure to crush the leaves somewhat. Fill the glass almost to the top with shaved ice, packing it down firmly. Pour in 3 tablespoons of bourbon and, with a long-handled bar spoon, use a chopping motion to mix it with the ice. Dry the outside of the glass and place it in the freezer for ½ hour. When served, the glass should be frosted and the ice inside almost solid.

"When removing the glass from the freezer, avoid touching the outside with the bare hands so that it remains frosted (use kitchen towels or a napkin). Garnish the drink with 2 slices of lemon, stick 2 sprigs of mint into the ice and sprinkle the mint with ½ teaspoon of confectioner's sugar. Sprinkle the sugar with 2 or 3 drops of brandy and serve with a long straw. Serve on a napkin so when the frost melts, it will not drip on the table."

"More people are driven insane through religious hysteria than by drinking alcohol." W. C. Fields (1880-1946)

Mojito

Tony Riddick, bartender at the Iguana Lounge in Phoenix, Arizona, said, "I didn't see him drink it but plenty of people have told me he did." Riddick is one of many who are aware that Hemingway lived in the Hotel Ambos Mundos in Havana and drank regularly at two bars. At El Floridita he drank a double daiquiri, which was named Papa Doble for him. At La Bodiguita del Medio he drank Mojito.

This old Cuban favorite drink must be made with particular ingredients, said Riddick. Riddick said a wooden stick to muddle or crush the mint leaves and sugar syrup to release mint oil is traditional.

He also suggested using quality rum like Gosling's Black Seal dark rum and Cruzan white rum. Riddick adds, rum is spelled with an "h" in the Caribbean, so it's "rhum."

- 1 slice lime
- 5 mint leaves, torn
- 1 ounce simple syrup (recipe below)
- 1 ounce white rum
- ½ ounce dark rum
- Splash of soda
- Mint sprig for garnish

Put lime slice, mint leaves and simple syrup in shaker glass and crush them together. Add rums, fill with ice and shake. Pour into rocks glass. Top off with ice and a splash of soda and garnish with mint sprig. Makes 1 drink.

Simple Syrup:
- 1 part water
- 1 part sugar
- Boil until thickened.

"When I'm old and gray, I want to have a house by the sea. And paint. With a lot of wonderful chums, good music and booze around. And a damn good kitchen to cook in." Ava Gardner (1922-1990)

Negroni

Alice B. Toklas (1877-1967) lover and publisher of Gertrude Stein wrote *The Alice B. Toklas Cookbook* and other works such as *Aromas and Flavors of Past and Present* and *What Is Remembered.* When she sent her first cookbook to the publisher in 1953, she wrote, "The Cookbook is finished and sent off and I'm coming to terms with my age-so that's that!"

She improved on Ford Madox Ford's "Americano" drink with the following addition of gin or vodka and named it "Negroni." She called it "heavenly."

- 1 part Campari
- 1 part red vermouth
- 1 part gin or vodka
- Ice
- Lemon slice
- Soda water, if desired for carbonation

Mix all and drink.

"There is something about an old-fashioned
That kindles a cardiac glow;
It is soothing and soft and impassioned
As a lyric by Swinburne or Poe.
There is something about an old-fashioned
When dusk has enveloped the sky,
And it may be the ice, or the pineapple slice,
But I strongly suspect it's the Rye."
Ogden Nash (1902-1971)

Old-Fashioned

Vincent Price's (1911-1993) surprising expertise in art and wonderful presence on *The $64,000 Challenge* led to his appearance on Edward R. Murrow's *Person to Person* television show. As his fame spread about his art knowledge, he decided to write a book about his interest in art called *I Like What I Know.* The title was a take-off on the frequent comment, "I know what I like."

Always one to look at things in a new way, he called this drink his "New Old-Fashioned." This recipe was on the Internet in an ad for Angostura Bitters.

- One sugar cube
- 3 dashes Angostura bitters
- A splash of club soda
- 2-3 ice cubes
- A lemon twist
- 1 maraschino cherry
- 1 ½ ounces light Canadian whiskey

Place all in a glass and stir.

"Away, away with rum, by gum
With rum, by gum, with rum, by gum
Away, away with rum, by gum;
The song of the Temperance Union."

Papa Doble

A. E. Hotchner, friend of Ernest Hemingway, Paul Newman, Gary Cooper, Lauren Bacall, and biographer of Doris Day, Sophia Loren and Hemingway described the Papa Doble. He said in *Papa Hemingway* that Ernest invented the Papa Doble at Sloppy Joe's Bar in Key West, Florida. He brought the idea from living in Havana and drinking them at the El Floridita bar near his hotel. Hemingway enjoyed this drink at Sloppy Joe's with Errol Flynn, Gary Cooper, Spencer Tracy and others.

Hemingway wrote *To Have and To Have Not* in Key West. He based the main character, played in the movie by Humphrey Bogart, on the owner of Sloppy Joe's. Joe used to take him fishing on his charter boat and that was the role Bogart played in the movie as captain of the Queen Conch charter fishing boat.

In the movie, the hero meets Lauren Bacall (Slim) in the local bar. In actuality, Hemingway met, fell in love, and married reporter Martha Gelhorn, who paid $20 to be introduced to the famous writer at Sloppy Joe's Bar. This recipe was available on the Internet.

- 2 ½ jiggers of white Bacardi rum
- Juice of 2 limes
- Juice from ½ grapefruit
- 6 drops of syrup from Maraschino cherries
- Shaved ice

Blend all ingredients in a mixer until foamy.

"I'm only a beer teetotaler, not a champagne teetotaler." George Bernard Shaw (1856-1950)

Peppered Champagne

Evelyn Waugh (1903-1966) was a major English satirist who began writing when he attended Oxford. He studied art and taught school but his interest in writing prompted him to become a reporter. He covered the Italo-Ethiopian War in 1935-1936. He then joined the Royal Marines during World War II and fought in North Africa, Crete and Yugoslavia.

Perhaps best known for *Brideshead Revisited,* he also wrote *Decline and Fall, Black Mischief, The Loved One* and other works. He once described this unusual version of champagne.

- 1 sugar cube
- Angostura Bitters
- Cayenne pepper
- Champagne

Waugh wrote: "He took a large tablet of beet sugar…and soaked it in Angostura Bitters and then rolled it in cayenne pepper. This he put into a large glass, which he filled up with champagne. Each bubble as it rises to the surface carries with it a red grain of pepper, so that as one drinks, one's appetite is at once stimulated and gratified, heat and cold, fire and liquid, contending on one's palate and alternating in the mastery of one's sensations, I sipped this almost unendurably desirable drink."

"Or from Browning some 'Pomegranate,'
Which, if cut deep down the middle,
Shows a heart within blood-tinctured
Of a veined humanity."
Elizabeth Barrett Browning (1806-1861)

Pomegranate Juice

The profound novelist Thomas Mann (1875-1955) was the son of a wealthy trader who had been elected burgomaster of Lubeck, Germany. Thomas first worked for a fire insurance company, then became a magazine writer and finally wrote his first important novel, *Buddenbrooks*. The citizens of Lubeck were outraged because they saw themselves being portrayed negatively in this book.

He studied philosophers and began to write with more depth, eventually completing such works as *Tonio Kroger; The Magic Mountain; Doctor Faustus;, Freud, Goethe and Wagner;* and *The Confessions of Felix Krull.* He won the Nobel Prize for Literature in 1929.

He wrote the exceptional *Death in Venice* in 1911. The scientist Aschenback visited Venice during the outbreak of cholera and found that he was strangely attracted to a young teenage boy. He tried to cool his passions and his fever with this drink but he would eventually die of the plague.

"Aschenback sat near the balustrade, a glass of pomegranate juice and soda water sparkling ruby red before him, with which he now and then moistened his lips. His nerves drank in thirstily the unlovely sounds, the vulgar and sentimental tunes, for passion paralyzes good taste and makes its victims accept with rapture what a man in his senses would either laugh at or turn from with disgust… Tadzio (the young Adonis) had long since left the balustrade. But he, the lonely man, sat for long, to the waiter's great annoyance, before the dregs of pomegranate juice in his glass."

"Bring in the bottled lightning, a clean tumbler, and a corkscrew." Charles Dickens (1812-1870)

Punch

John Steinbeck (1902-1968) grew up in Salinas, California, where his father was county treasurer and his mother was a teacher. He studied marine biology at Stanford and worked as a laborer, fruit picker, and reporter.

As he began to write, he mixed in ideas from Jungian psychology, Joseph Campbell mythology, and his own tireless championing of the rights of migrant workers. He wrote *Tortilla Flat, The Red Pony, The Pearl, East of Eden, Of Mice and Men, The Grapes of Wrath, Travels With Charley, The Winter of Our Discontent*, and wrote the screenplay for the movie *Viva Zapata*. He won the Nobel Prize for Literature in 1962.

He also wrote about San Francisco's *Cannery Row*. Among his characters was a substitute bartender at La Ida named Eddie who created an interesting "punch."

"He kept a gallon jug under the bar and in the mouth of the jug there was a funnel. Anything left in the glasses Eddie poured into the funnel before he washed the glasses. If an argument or a song were going on at La Ida, or late at night when good fellowship had reached its logical conclusion, Eddie poured glasses half or two-thirds full into the funnel. The resulting punch which he took back to the hotel was always interesting and sometimes surprising. The mixture of rye, beer, bourbon, scotch, wine, rum and gin was fairly constant, but now and then some effete customer would order a stinger or an anisette or a curacao and these little touches gave a distinct character to the punch.

It was Eddie's habit always to shake a little angostura into the jug just before he left. It was a source of satisfaction to him that nobody was out anything. He had observed that a man got just as drunk on half a glass as on a whole one, if he was in the mood to get drunk at all."

"Twas a woman drove me to drink, and I never had the courtesy to thank her for it." W. C. Fields (1880-1946)

Ramos Fizz

Morton Thompson (?-1953), who wrote *Not As A Stranger* and other books enjoyed drinking this while he made his famous Black Turkey (See Chapter on Black Turkey).

- 4 egg whites
- Equal amount of whipping cream
- Juice of half a lemon less 1 teaspoon
- ½ teaspoon confectioners sugar
- Amount of gin according to taste
- Ice cubes
- 2 tablespoons club soda
- Dash of orange flower water

Mix the first four ingredients in a mixer. Add the gin, ice, soda and flower water.

"I love to drink martinis
Two at the very most.
Three, I'm under the table,
Four, I'm under the host."
Dorothy Parker (1893-1967)

Roosevelt Martini

Franklin D. Roosevelt (1882-1945) before and during his presidency gave historic speeches, fireside chats, proclamations, and documents that changed U.S. history. He also wrote *Crisis at the White House* and *The Political Arena.*

According to Barnaby Conrad III, F.D.R. loved martinis and served one to Stalin at the 1943 Teheran Conference. One person called the U.S. Soviet relations under FDR the "four martinis and let's have an agreement." Roosevelt called Stalin's caviar gifts "Uncle Joe's Bounty." This description and recipe was available on the Internet.

- Two parts gin
- One part vermouth
- 1 teaspoon of olive brine
- Lemon peel
- Olive

Shake with ice, strain and pour into a glass after rubbing the rim with lemon peeling. Serve with an olive.

"So we grew together,
Like to a double cherry, seeming parted,
But yet an union in partition;
Two lovely berries molded on one stem."
William Shakespeare (1564-1616)

Singapore Sling

This drink, invented by the Long Bar at the Raffles Hotel in Singapore, became famous when writers such as Joseph Conrad (1857-1924) and Somerset Maugham (1874-1965) described it. This recipe was available on the Internet.

- 2 parts dry gin
- 1 part cherry brandy
- 1 part fresh lemon juice
- Soda water
- Slice of lemon
- Maraschino cherry

Place four ice cubes in a cocktail shaker and add the gin, brandy and lemon juice. Shake well and strain into a highball glass. Top with soda water and garnish with the slice of lemon and a cherry on a cocktail stick.

"Claret is the liquor for boys; port for men; but he would aspires to be a hero must drink brandy." Samuel Johnson (1709-1784)

Stinger

Ian Fleming, who wrote the James Bond 007 series, greatly admired Evelyn Waugh. In *Diamonds Are Forever*, Bond drinks Waugh's signature "Stinger". This recipe was available on the Internet.

- 1 ½ ounce brandy
- ½ ounce white crème de menthe

Shake ingredients with ice, and strain into a cocktail glass.

"Be careful crossing streets, oo-oo!
Don't eat meats, oo-oo!
Cut out sweets, oo-oo!
You'll get a pain and ruin your tum-tum!
Keep away from bootleg hooch
When you're on a spree.
Take good care of yourself, you belong to me."
G. DeSylva, Lew Brown and Ray Henderson

Turkey Cocktail

F. Scott Fitzgerald (1896-1940) was named for an ancestor, Francis Scott Key. His father was a salesman and his mother inherited money from her Irish Catholic immigrant father who supported the family. He attended a prep school, then Princeton, but spent more time writing song lyrics and humorous pieces than studying. Unlikely to graduate, he joined the army in 1917. Thinking he would die in the war, he hurriedly wrote *The Romantic Egotist*. Editors told him that if he revised it, it showed promise.

In military camp he fell in love with Zelda, a southern belle. As he was unable to support her, she broke it off. After his success with *This Side of Paradise*, she married him. They lived lavishly in the U.S. and in Paris and he survived by writing commercial stories for the *Saturday Evening Post*. They went into debt, argued and drank heavily. When he wrote *The Great Gatsby*, they recovered financially but Zelda began to be mentally ill. His last important novel was *Tender Is the Night*.

After Zelda's hospitalization, he moved to Hollywood to write screenplays and fell in love with Sheila Graham. He died while working on the half-finished *The Love of the Last Tycoon*. He had a unique recipe for a turkey cocktail which reflected his own battle with alcohol.

"To one large turkey, add one gallon of vermouth and a demijohn of Angostura bitters. Shake."

"Adde sugar, nutmeg and ginger
With store of ale too;
And thus ye must do
To make a Wassaile a swinger."
Robert Herrick

Wassail

Robert Herrick (1591-1674) was known as one of England's "Cavalier Poets." He wrote over 1300 short musical lyrics, poems, books, and other kinds of works. Now his quotations are better known than the names of his works. For example, he wrote "Gather ye rosebuds while ye may."

This recipe comes from the poem quoted above. Since ginger rhymed with swinger, the latter word clearly does not have the same meaning it does today. However, with enough wassail, one might become a swinger.

- 1 ½ pounds apples, cored
- 1 quart ale
- 1 tablespoon or more sugar
- 1/8 teaspoon each, ground ginger and nutmeg

Preheat the oven to 375 degrees. Bake the apples in a large dish for 45 minutes, or until they burst. Set them aside to cool. When they are cool enough to handle, remove the peel and mash the pulp. This should make about 1 ½ cups.

In a large pot, heat the ale. With a whisk, blend the apple pulp, sugar and spices. Adjust seasonings to taste. Place the mixture in a heat proof bowl and sprinkle the top with some additional nutmeg.

Chapter 3

SALADS

My Dear, How Ever Did You Think Up This Delicious Salad?"

This is a very sad ballad,
Because it's about the way too many people make a salad.
Generally they start with bananas,
And they might just as well use gila monsters or iguanas.
Pineapples are another popular ingredient,
Although there is one school that holds
Preserved pears or peaches more expedient,
And you occasionally meet your fate
In the form of a prune or a date.
Rarely you may chance to discover a soggy piece
Of tomato looking very forlorn and Cinderella-ry,
But for the most part you are confronted by apples and celery,
And it's not a bit of use at this point to turn pale
Or break out in a cold perspiration,
Because all this is only the foundation,
Because if you think the foundation sounds unenticing,
Just wait until we get to the dressing, or rather, the icing.
There are various methods of covering up the body,

48

And to some, marshmallows are the pall supreme,
And others prefer whipped cream,
And then they deck the grave with
Ground-up peanuts and maraschinos
And you get the effect of a funeral like Valentino's
And about the only thing
That in this kind of salad is never seen
Is any kind of green,
And oil and vinegar and salt and pepper are at a minimum,
But there is a maximum of sugar and syrup
And ginger and nutmeg and cinnamum.
Ogden Nash (1902-1971)

"Our Garrick's a salad for in him we see
Oil, vinegar, sugar and saltness agree.
Oliver Goldsmith (1730-1774) describing the great actor, Garrick

Caesar Salad

Vincent Price (1911-1993), best known as an actor, wrote *I Like What I Know, The Book of Joe, A Treasury of Great Recipes*, and other works.

He starred in many movies such as *The Tower of London, The House of Seven Gables, The Song of Bernadette, Wilson, Laura, Keys of the Kingdom, Leave Her to Heaven, The Three Musketeers, House of Wax, The Ten Commandments, The Fly* and *Edward Scissorhands*. He called this recipe "Vincent Price's Caesar Salad for a Busy Cook." This recipe is available on the Internet.

- 2 heads romaine lettuce, washed, dried
- 1 clove garlic, peeled
- ¾ cup olive oil
- Dash cayenne pepper
- Dash Tabasco sauce
- 1 teaspoon sugar
- 1 10"-strip anchovy paste
- Freshly ground black pepper
- ½ teaspoon salt
- 1 egg
- 1 large lemon, juiced
- Freshly grated Parmesan cheese
- Croutons

Place the peeled garlic clove in olive oil in a container with a tight-fitting lid; set aside overnight. Remove and discard garlic from oil; add cayenne, Tabasco, sugar and anchovy paste. Shake well to mix; set aside. Tear the lettuce leaves into smaller pieces and place in a large salad bowl. Sprinkle with salt and pepper. Pour the seasoned oil over all and toss gently so that all leaves are well coated.

Boil the egg for 1 minute (bring water to a boil, lower egg into water with a large spoon and begin timing.) Crack the shell and drop egg into salad. Squeeze lemon juice over egg and stir gently into salad. It will have a creamy appearance. Just before serving, sprinkle cheese over all and add croutons. Toss lightly to mix.

Note: Since this recipe contains a partially cooked egg, if concerned about salmonella, substitute an equivalent amount of Egg Beaters or other egg substitute.

"Celery, raw, develops the jaw,
But celery stewed, is more quietly chewed."
Ogden Nash (1902-1971)

Celery with Parmesan

Dr. Diane Holloway, psychologist, writer, and editor of this book, enjoyed living and marrying in Paris, France in the late 1950s. She used to frequent those cafes described in the books of Ernest Hemingway. One of these was called Deux Magots (Two Maggots) on the Left Bank. She came to love this recipe, as had many of the 1920s and 1930s literati who mingled there.

- 4 cups celery cut in 1 inch pieces
- chicken or veal stock

- ½ teaspoon salt
- 2 tablespoons butter
- ½ cup grated Parmesan cheese
- Dash ground white pepper

Place celery in a saucepan and pour in boiling stock and salt to a depth of ½ inch. Cover, bring to boiling point, and cook 10 minutes or only until celery is crisp-tender. Drain, add butter, half the cheese, and pepper. Toss. Serve with remaining cheese sprinkled on top. Makes 6 servings.

"One cantaloupe is ripe and lush
Another's green, another's mush.
I'd buy a lot more cantaloupe
If I possessed a fluoroscope."
Ogden Nash (1902-1971)

Joy's Fruit Salad

Nancy L. Snyderman, M.D., a physician of television fame, described Joy's Fruit Salad.

"As I reflect on the makings of a great Girls' Night Out, I quickly realize the list is short and succinct: Joy's Fruit Salad, some Chardonnay, sourdough baguettes, and friends who are women folk… We always gather at somebody's house, but not on a regularly scheduled basis. When it's my house for Girls' Night Out, I serve the fruit salad I grew up with: the one my mother, Joy, made all year round."

"For Joy's Fruit Salad, mix any fruit with low-fat or nonfat vanilla yogurt. Never use fruits that are not in season—this makes them more exciting when they are available. For example, use lots of honeydew melons, cantaloupes, strawberries, and grapes in the summer… Since becoming an adult, I also add gorgonzola and walnuts."

"Mayonnaise: One of the sauces which serve the French in place of a state religion." Ambrose Bierce (1842-1914)

Lobster, Chicken Truffle Salad

Alice B. Toklas, pianist, writer, art lover and producer of Gertrude Stein works was a great cook. Those who visited the Toklas-Stein salon in Paris included Ernest Hemingway, John Steinbeck, Truman Capote, Ford Madox Ford, F. Scott Fitzgerald, Cowley, Pound, Jean Cocteau, James Joyce, Sherwood Anderson, Pablo Picasso, T. S. Eliot, Frank Harris, Henry Miller, E. E. Cummings, and many others.

Alice loved to include Truffles in her recipes. However, they are terribly rare and very expensive. Some cooks prefer to substitute other mushrooms for them. This recipe contains a rather outrageous combination of foods for a buffet platter and all of them do not have to be included to still have a matchless presentation.

- Virgin olive oil
- White wine vinegar
- 4 tablespoons turkey broth
- ½ teaspoon tarragon mustard
- Lobster meat
- Salt and pepper
- Sliced chicken breast
- Sliced turkey breast

- Sliced partridge breast
- Sliced truffles (cooked in wine)
- Sliced mushrooms
- Shrimp or crawfish
- Escarole or endive leaves
- Sliced ham
- 1 tablespoon capers in white wine
- 1 cup green olives pitted
- Tower of mayonnaise
- Dry champagne

Pour into a salad bowl the best olive oil, white wine vinegar, 4 table-spoons juice of turkey broth, tarragon/mustard, salt and pepper and mix with the lobster. Then add seafood and other meats, arranging in layers over leaves around a tower of mayonnaise with the largest truffle on top of the tower. Scatter capers and olives over all and serve with the best dry champagne available.

"It's certain that fine women eat
A crazy salad with their meat."
Rudyard Kipling (1865-1936)

Overnight Layered Salad

Phyllis Orsi organizes events for writers and students in the Phoenix area where Erma Bombeck (1927–1996) lived. Phyllis contributed this spectacular Bombeck salad recipe. Erma wrote humorous newspaper syndicated columns and books despite suffering from terminal kidney failure for the last several years of her life.

Bombeck wrote *Family Ties That Bind and Gag, If Life Is a Bowl of Cherries What Am I Doing in the Pits? The Grass Is Always Greener Over the Septic Tank, I Lost Everything in the Post Natal Depression, Forever Erma,* and other wonderful books.

- 1 medium head lettuce, shredded
- ½ cup green onions, chopped
- 1 can water chestnuts, drained, sliced
- 1 10-ounce package frozen peas
- 2 cups mayonnaise
- 1 cup celery, thinly sliced
- 2 teaspoons sugar
- ½ cup grated Parmesan cheese
- ½ teaspoon each, salt and pepper
- ½ teaspoon garlic powder
- 3 hard boiled eggs, chopped fine
- 1 cup crisp crumbled bacon
- 1 ½ cups tomatoes, cut in 1 inch wedges

Place lettuce in a 9" x 13" glass dish. Top with onions, celery and water chestnuts. Break pea package and spread over for next layer. Spread mayonnaise on top. Sprinkle on sugar, salt, pepper, garlic powder, and Parmesan. Cover with plastic wrap and refrigerate for 12 hours.

Just before serving, sprinkle eggs and bacon on top. Then garnish with fresh tomato wedges. To serve, cut in squares, use spatula to lift out. Serves 8.

"Eat no onions nor garlic, for we are to utter sweet breath." William Shakespeare (1564-1619)

Pinto Bean Salad

Willa Cather (1876-1947) graduated from the University of Nebraska and became a journalist, teacher and critic. She wrote reviews for a Pittsburgh newspaper, and left to become a high school teacher. Later she traveled to Europe, published poems and short stories, and finally became managing editor of New York magazine. She met many writers and never married.

She wrote *O Pioneers, My Antonia, One of Ours,* and *Death Comes For the Archbishop.* The latter was set in Santa Fe. For French Father Latour's first Christmas in Santa Fe, he rode 3,000 miles on horseback for religious reasons, and gathered the ingredients for a soup and salad he wanted to serve.

He then stated, "A bean salad was the best I could do for you; but with onion, and just a suspicion of salt pork, it is not so bad." His ingredients included these plus some optional possibilities from plants that grew around Santa Fe.

- Cooked pinto beans
- Diced salt pork
- Chopped onions
- Minced garlic cloves
- Good olive oil
- Salt and pepper
- Optional: cumin, lemon juice, cilantro, greens

"Papa, potatoes, poultry, prunes and prism, are all very good words for the lips; especially prunes and prism." Charles Dickens (1812-1870)

Potato Salad

Alexander Dumas (1802-1870) was most famous for his adventure stories such as *The Three Musketeers, The Count of Monte Cristo* and many more. He also wrote a book called *Spanish Cuisine.*

This potato salad, although slightly modified, has some of his interesting differences from the usual recipes. This recipe is available on the Internet.

- 8-9 potatoes
- 1 ½ cup dry white wine
- ½ cup chopped green onion
- ½ cup shredded carrots
- ¾ cup olive oil
- 3 tablespoons wine vinegar
- Salt and pepper
- ½ cup slivered toasted almonds
- 4 tablespoons mayonnaise
- 3 boiled eggs, sliced
- 2 tablespoons parsley, chopped

Boil potatoes until pierceable. Then peel them and break them apart. Pour the white wine over them and cool them. Add onion, carrots, oil, vinegar, salt and pepper. Chill until ready to serve, then toss with mayonnaise, garnish with almonds, eggs, and parsley.

"If you are lucky enough to have lived in Paris as a young man, then wherever you go for the rest of your life, it stays with you, for Paris is a moveable feast."
Ernest Hemingway (1899-1961)

Mary Hemingway's Seviche

This recipe came from Susan and Peter Buckley, friends of Mary and Ernest Hemingway. Susan remembered enjoying this recipe at Mary's apartment in New York but believes Mary first prepared it aboard *Pilar*, the Hemingway yacht.

Pilar was the older Spanish woman in *For Whom the Bell Tolls* who took over when her husband was ostracized from the revolutionary group for treason. The character of Pilar was probably based on Ernest's friend, Gertrude Stein, a strong woman who said, like Pilar, "I would have made a good man."

Peter Buckley became a bullfight lover and wrote *Bullfight* as well as *Ernest*, his biography of Hemingway. This recipe is available on the Internet.

- 1 pound fresh cod, halibut, scallops or shelled shrimp
- ¾ cup freshly squeezed lime juice
- ¼ cup chopped fresh coriander
- ½ cup sliced red onions (optional)
- ¼ teaspoon chopped hot pepper or dash Tabasco

Mix all ingredients together and marinate in the refrigerator for at least an hour. Seviche can be kept for up to 24 hours, but it's best eaten within a few hours. 4 servings.

Chapter 4

SOUPS

To Tip or Not To Tip a Soup Bowl

On the subject of whether or not to tip a soup bowl to get the last drops of soup, Will Rogers (1879-1935) responded to a New York drama critic who criticized him for suggesting that people should not tip their soup bowls.

"You say you learned to eat soup from a head waiter in the Middle West. Well, I admit my ignorance again; I never saw a headwaiter eat soup. Down in Oklahoma where I come from, we wouldn't let a head-waiter eat at our table, even if we had a headwaiter, which we haven't. If I remember right I think it was my mother taught me what little she knew of how I should eat, because if we had had to wait until we sent and got a head waiter to show us, we would have all starved to death... As bad as you plate tippers want all you can get, you don't want it in your lap.... The question of the World today is, not how to eat soup, but how to get soup to eat."

"But I always felt that I'd rather be a provincial hot tamale than soup without seasoning." F. Scott Fitzgerald (1896-1940)

Andaluz Gazpacho

According to Alice B. Toklas, among the many gazpachos were some particularly suited to the area around Andaluz. This is one of the many recipes she collected for her cookbook after Gertrude Stein died.

- 4 large tomatoes
- 1 cucumber, sliced
- 1 medium onion, sliced
- 1 medium green pepper, sliced
- 2 cloves garlic
- 3 eggs, beaten
- Dash cayenne
- ¼ cup vinegar
- ½ cup virgin olive oil
- 1 cup thick tomato juice
- Salt and pepper to taste
- 1 cup bread cubes
- 1 cup diced cucumber
- ¾ cup diced green pepper
- ½ cup chopped onion
- Chopped parsley

Puree the tomatoes, sliced cucumber, onion, green pepper, and 1 clove garlic a little at a time in a blender or food processor. Add eggs, cayenne, vinegar, ¼ cup oil, juice, salt and pepper. Mix well and chill. Crush remaining clove garlic, add to remaining ¼ cup oil, and brown the bread cubes in this oil. Add to the soup along with diced cucumber, diced green pepper, and chopped onion just before serving. Sprinkle chopped parsley on each serving. Serves 8.

"Soup of the evening, beautiful soup!" Lewis Carroll (1832-1898)

Asparagus Soup

Emile Zola (1840-1902) grew up in a poor household after the early death of his father, and his mother lived on a small pension. He failed an exam to enter law school so became a clerk in a shipping firm, a salesman for a Parisian publishing company, and began to write political and literary columns. A rash autobiographical piece got him fired. He then wrote a series of books about a money-driven family. He tried to taste the lives of those he wrote about.

In *Nana*, he wrote about prostitution. In *Germinal* he wrote about the mining industry. In *L'Assommoir (The Drunk)* he wrote about the Parisian working class. His letter to a newspaper called *J'Accuse* reopened the Jewish Dreyfus case and he was sentenced to prison for this attack, but escaped. When the case was resolved, he returned to Paris where he became known as the developer of the "natural" style of writing.

Zola's books showed the plight of the disadvantaged lower working class, who often survived by eating soup such as this recipe, which was created by him or for him. He described the old market section (Les Halles) where one would buy asparagus as the "belly of Paris." This recipe is available on the Internet.

- ¾ kilo asparagus, trimmed
- 1 ¼ cup butter
- 1/3 cup flour
- 5 cups chicken stock
- Salt and pepper
- 4 egg yolks
- ¼ cup cream
- Pinch of sugar

Place the asparagus in a large saucepan and pour enough water to cover. Bring to a boil then reduce the heat. Simmer until the tips are tender. Drain, cut off the tender tips and set them aside.

Cut the remaining stalks of the asparagus into ½ to 1 inch pieces. In a saucepan, melt half the butter and cook the stalks in it.

In a separate saucepan melt all but 1 tablespoon of the remaining butter. First stir the flour into this melted butter and gradually stir in the chicken stock. Simmer gently for five minutes.

Pour about ½ cup of the stock mixture over the asparagus stalks and then liquidize this in a blender or food processor to have an asparagus puree. Pour this through a strainer into the rest of the stock. Reheat the mixture on a low heat and season with salt and pepper.

In a mixing bowl, beat the egg yolks with the cream. Gradually pour ½ cup of the hot soup into this while whipping with a wire whisk to prevent the eggs from curdling. Pour this mixture into the soup, heat over a moderate flame without boiling for 5 minutes.

Add a pinch of sugar and salt and pepper to taste.

Add the asparagus tips and heat through. Immediately before serving, float the remaining butter on top of the soup. Serves 4-6.

"We owe much to the fruitful meditation of our sages, but a sane view of life is, after all, elaborated mainly in the kitchen." Joseph Conrad (1857-1924)

Beef Soup

Thomas Jefferson (1743-1826) was interested in everything. When he sent Lewis and Clark to explore the area west of the Mississippi River, he told them to record everything and send or bring home flora and fauna. He grew his own creative gardens in Monticello, the mansion where he invented many home aids like the dumb waiter.

He was a prolific writer and created most of *The Declaration of Independence* as well as writing a very interesting document called *The Life and Morals of Jesus of Nazareth.*

He gave these instructions to those who would make his Beef Soup.

"Always observe to lay your meat in the bottom of the pan with a lump of butter. Cut the herbs and vegetables very fine and lay over the meat. Cover it close and set over a slow fire. This will draw the virtue out of the herbs and roots and give the soup a different flavor from what it would have from putting the water in at first. When the gravy produced from the meat is almost dried up, fill your pan with water. When your soup is done, take it up and when cool enough, skim off the grease quite clean. Put it on again to heat and then dish it up."

"Give them great meals of beef and iron and steel,
They will eat like wolves and fight like devils."
William Shakespeare (1564-1619)

Beef Stew

William Sidney Porter, alias O. Henry (1862-1910) was the son of a physician but his mother died when he was three. He was raised in North Carolina by his grandmother and aunt who put him in her school where he learned to love books. He became a licensed pharmacist but went to Texas for his health. There he worked on a sheep ranch for a family friend, became a draftsman (he had enjoyed sketching and cartoons) and he later became a bank teller in Austin, Texas.

He wrote a column for the Houston Daily Post and founded a humor weekly which quickly failed. He took to drink and had marital problems and then was accused of embezzlement by his bank. First he fled the country but returned when he learned his wife was dying. He was sentenced to five years and served three, worked in the prison pharmacy, and wrote short stories to support his daughter.

He used the name O. Henry to disguise his real identity and when paroled, went to New York. There, he wrote wonderful short stories, which usually had an ironic twist ending, and his works included "The Ransom of Red Chief", "The Gift of the Magi" and "The Third Ingredient."

In the latter story, O. Henry's third ingredient was an onion. The protagonist encountered a man with an onion in the hall and said this to him.

"Raw onion is a mighty poor diet. And so is a beef stew without one. There's a little lady, a friend of mine, in my room there at the end of the hall. Both of us are out of luck; and we had just potatoes and meat between us. They're stewing now. But it ain't got any soul. There's something lacking to it. There's certain things in life that are naturally intended to fit and belong together. One is pink cheesecloth and green roses; and one is ham and eggs, and one is Irish and trouble. And the other is beef and potatoes with onions."

"Let us have wine and women, mirth and laughter,
Sermons and soda water the day after."
George Gordon, Lord Byron (1788-1824)

Bouillabaisse

William Makepeace Thackeray (1811-1863) was born in Calcutta but educated in England. After attending Trinity College, he studied law but when he lost his inheritance, he resorted to writing. He traveled abroad and wrote *Paris Sketchbook, Irish Sketchbook, The History of Henry Esmond,* contributed to *Punch,* and wrote *Vanity Fair.*

He dabbled in poetry and wrote about bouillabaisse in a magazine. Some verses of "The Ballad of Bouillabaisse" are these, and later verses include the burgundy and claret that he enjoyed with this soup.

"This Bouillabaisse a noble dish is
A sort of soup, or broth or brew,
Or hotchpotch of all sorts of fishes,
That Greenwich never could outdo:
Green herbs, red peppers, mussels, saffron,
Soles, onion, garlic, roach and dace:
All these you eat at Terre's tavern
In that one dish of Bouillabaisse."

"I'm the President and I don't have to eat broccoli." George Bush, Sr.

Broccoli Soup

Jean Homme, short story writer, retired to Sun City, Arizona, from Minneapolis, Minnesota. She was an insurance and law secretary for 47 years. She has written four short stories and had one piece, "Christmas Angels" published in the Daily News Sun on December 25, 2001.

- 5 ounces chopped broccoli
- ¼ cup chopped onion
- 1 ½ tablespoon butter
- ¼ cup flour
- 1 can 14.5 ounces chicken broth
- ½ cup milk
- 1/8 teaspoon black pepper
- 1/8 teaspoon ground red pepper
- 1/8 teaspoon ground thyme
- ¼ teaspoon salt

Cook the broccoli for three minutes in the microwave if you want to take a shortcut. In a soup pot, sauté the onion in butter until it turns putrid yellow. Add the flour and stir to blend. Add chicken broth, milk, pepper, red pepper, thyme, salt and broccoli. Cook and stir until thick and smooth. Your mother will be proud of you for eating this dish.

"An idealist is one who, on noticing that roses smell better than a cabbage, concludes that it will also make better soup." H. L. Mencken (1880-1956)

Cabbage Soup

Jean Homme, short story writer, retired to Sun City, Arizona, from Minneapolis, Minnesota.

- ½ head cabbage
- 2 ribs of celery
- 6 green onions
- ¼ red pepper, seeded
- 1 10 ounce can Rotel tomatoes and chilies
- ½ package onion soup OR
- 1 can beef broth OR 2 beef bouillon cubes
- 1 can 14.5 ounces, diced tomatoes OR
- 16 ounce can of V-8 juice

Put on an old-fashioned apron and dice cabbage, celery, onions and red pepper, whacking them. Place them in a large pot and cover with water, and cover the pot. With a lid, of course. Boil rapidly for ten minutes. Then add the Rotel tomatoes, onion soup, and diced tomatoes, simmering for ½ hour.

This serves four self-disciplined eaters, or two who skipped breakfast. It is tasty, fat free, practically calorie free and freezes well. You can remove your apron now.

"Training is everything. The peach was once a bitter almond; cauliflower is nothing but cabbage with a college education." Mark Twain (1835-1910)

Cauliflower Soup

Victoria Wood, British comedian and writer is, unfortunately, hardly known outside Great Britain. She has written numerous comedy skits, songs, television shows, and theater productions including the current *Dinner Ladies.* She won "Writer of the Year" in 2000 for British television.

Her recipe combines potato with the cauliflower, adding a good bit of body to the soup. This recipe is available on the Internet.

- 1 potato
- 1 onion
- 1 cauliflower
- 1 ounce butter
- 1 pint vegetable stock
- 1 pint milk
- Salt and pepper

Chop the potato and onion. Heat the butter and add the chopped vegetables and sauté. Cut off cauliflower florets and add to the sauté. Add the stock, boil and simmer for 20 minutes. Then add the milk. Blend in a food processor. Add the seasonings. Reheat as needed before serving.

Edited by Diane Holloway, Ph.D. • 69

*"I'm Popeye the sailor man
I'm Popeye the sailor man
I'm strong to the finich,
Cause I eats me spinach."*

Chicken Soup

David H. Citron is a technical writer, journalist, copywriter, web author and wrote a recipe like he would write a technical manual. This recipe is available on the Internet on Citron's web site. He suggests additions like spinach and vegetables, which makes this a more interesting chicken soup. This writing style for recipes is quite unique.

Minimum hardware and software requirements for an instance of almost homemade store-bought canned chicken soup include the following:
Hardware:
- A stovetop, with gas, electric or equivalent processor.
- One each, pot and mixing spoon.
- Utensil required for opening soup container.
- A quantity of soup bowls and spoons greater than or equal to the number of guests plus one for yourself.

Software:
- A can or envelope of your favorite canned chicken soup or broth mix and the appropriate amount of water, per package instructions.
- Up to half of an 8 ounce bag or box of your favorite uncooked egg noodles or pasta of your choice or even the equivalent amount of frozen wontons from the Chinese grocery store, if there's one nearby.
- Hint: In a pinch, ravioli, tortelli, or kreplach may be substituted for wontons. *Don't worry! No one will notice the difference!*

- Up to a cup of cut up leftover cooked chicken, from which you have removed bones and skin. (How to do so is beyond the scope of this document.)
- A few stalks of fresh dill, cut up small, or a few tablespoons of dried dill weed.
- Whatever leftover cooked vegetables you'd like to add. If you add scallions or spinach (as in wonton soup), DON'T cook them in advance!
- Optional: If you want it to taste more like wonton soup, add a small amount (up to half a teaspoon) of oriental sesame oil, from the gourmet section of the grocery store. (It's dark brown.) Don't get health-food-type sesame oil. It's pale, and not the same.

Instructions for Almost Homemade Store-Bought Canned Chicken Soup

1. In a large pot, cook noodles or pasta per directions, a few minutes shy of the recommended cooking time.
2. Drain the noodles/pasta and return them to the pot. Make sure the strainer has holes that are smaller than the pasta.
3. Open the can/envelope of soup with an electric or manual can opener or scissors or other appropriate sharp instrument, after reading directions for that implement and taking all safety precautions. **Warning:** Do not run with scissors. You could put an eye out!
4. Add the soup concentrate to the cooked noodles/pasta in the pot.
5. Add the required amount of water, per package or can instructions. You may want to add up to (estimated) 30% more water than the recipe calls for, because those noodles will absorb more moisture. Use your judgment.
6. Add chicken, and the vegetables, if any. **Exception:** Save scallions and/or spinach to add later. **Warning:** Do not add salt.

Canned soup and mixes are usually already too salty. Pepper or Mrs. Dash, maybe.

7. While you wait for the soup to come to a boil, add the dill. Stir frequently, so the noodles don't stick to the bottom of the pot and burn.

8. Let the soup boil briefly, just long enough to make sure it is heated thoroughly. Consider the size of the pieces of meat. **Hint:** Now's the time to add the optional scallions and/or spinach, if desired.

9. Serve the soup in large bowls, with soupspoons or tablespoons. **Hint:** Put salt, pepper and Mrs. Dash on the table, so diners can decide what to add.

10. Eat the soup.

11. Place the leftovers, if any, in an appropriate container and refrigerate promptly.

12. Contact technical writer David H. Citron about writing your user manuals, brochures, online documents, web pages or recipes.

"Things are seldom what they seem
Skim milk masquerades as cream."
Sir William S. Gilbert (1836-1911) from *H.M.S. Pinafore*

Clam Chowder

Herman Melville (1819-1891) was born in New York City to a merchant. His father became bankrupt, insane, and died when he was 12. His mother had to raise eight children and Herman went to work as a clerk and farmhand at the age of 12. Later he became a cabin boy and then joined the U.S. Navy. He sailed to Honolulu, Tahiti, and Typee. He wrote *Typee* about the cannibals, *Omoo* and then *Moby Dick* in 1851. Nathaniel Hawthorne said he should turn *Moby Dick* into an allegory, which he did, but it did not achieve popularity until Melville was dead. In his latter years he worked as a customs inspector and wrote *Bartleby the Scrivener* and left *Billy Budd* unfinished. He is most famous for *Moby Dick* in which he described a wonderful clam chowder that lends itself to this recipe.

"Queequeg, said I, "do you think that we can make out a supper for us both on one clam? However, a warm savory steam from the kitchen served to belie the apparently cheerless prospect before us. But when that smoking chowder came in, the mystery was delightfully explained. O sweet friends! Harken to me. It was made of small juicy clams, scarcely bigger than hazel nuts, mixed with pounded ship biscuit, and salted pork cut up into little flakes; the whole poached with butter and plentifully seasoned with pepper and salt."

- 2 slices of bacon
- 1 onion, chopped
- 1 cup of celery and leaves, chopped
- ½ tablespoon of flour
- 2 cups of fish stock
- 2 white potatoes, diced (if ship biscuit is unavailable)
- 1 teaspoon of seafood seasoning
- 1 cup of milk
- 1 cup of whipping cream
- 12-13 ounces of canned chopped clams

Fry bacon in a large saucepan. When crisp, take out the bacon. Put the onion and celery in the grease and sauté until translucent. Stir in the flour, then pour in the fish stock and stir till it's thickened. Dump in the potatoes and seafood seasoning, bring to a boil, cover, turn down the heat and simmer for 20 minutes.

Add the milk, cream, clams, and clam liquid, then take it off the fire until you're ready to serve it. When it's time to eat, heat through, ladle into big bowls, and crumble the bacon on top.

"A cucumber should be well sliced, and dressed with pepper and vinegar, and then thrown out, as good for nothing." Samuel Johnson (1709-1784)

Cold Cucumber Soup

Hemingway's mother, Grace, published this recipe in *The Nineteenth Century Women's Club Historical Centennial Cookbook.* It was also published in Craig Boreth's 1998 book, *The Hemingway Cookbook.*

Hemingway was strongly influenced by both his mother and his father, who were extremely religious. He was interested in older women and his first wife was eight years older than himself. After he had an affair, they divorced but he dedicated *The Sun Also Rises* to Hadley (his older wife) and his son. They were to receive the royalties also.

Boreth's cookbook has very interesting commentary and recipes including Nick Adams' streamside coffee and Hemingway's Fillet of Lion. This soup recipe is available on the Internet.

- 3 cucumbers
- 1 tablespoon butter
- 1 tablespoon chopped fresh dill or mint
- 1 leek, white part only, sliced, or ¼ cup
- Chopped onion

- 1 bay leaf
- 1 tablespoon all purpose flour
- 2 cups fresh chicken stock or canned broth
- 1 teaspoon salt, or to taste
- White pepper (optional)
- 1 cup half and half
- Juice of ½ lemon
- 1 tablespoon honey (optional)

Peel and slice two of the cucumbers. Peel, seed and grate the remaining cucumber. Heat the butter in a saucepan. Add the cucumbers and cook on low for a few minutes. Add the dill or mint, leek and bay leaf and cook over low fire until tender, about 20 minutes.

Stir in the flour and cook a few more minutes, stirring constantly.

Add the stock and salt and simmer for 30 minutes. Remove the bay leaf and let it cool slightly. Puree the mixture, half at a time, in a blender or food processor. Return to the pan and add the white pepper. Add the half and half, lemon juice and honey. Taste and adjust the seasoning. Stir in the grated cucumber.

Refrigerate until ready to serve. Serve in a chilled bowl. 4-6 servings.

"There are five elements: earth, air, fire, water and garlic." Louis Diat (1885-1957)

Garlic Soup

Philosopher George Santayana (1863-1952) was born in Madrid and moved to Boston in 1872. He was educated at Harvard, where he became professor of philosophy, while retaining his Spanish nationality. He began writing poems and sonnets, but later became known as a philosopher and stylist. He wrote a 5-volume *The Life of Reason,* the 4-volume *Realms of Being,* and a novel called *The Last Puritan.*

He moved to Europe in 1912, stayed in Oxford during WWI, then settled in Rome. He described his love for Garlic Soup, a Spanish dish, in *Persons and Places: The Background of My Life.* This recipe is available on the Internet.

"The Spanish dignity in humility was most marked in my father. He lived when necessary and almost by preference like the poor, without the least comfort, variety or entertainment… For supper they had each a bowl of garlic soup, something that my father loved in his old age, and that I also liked, especially if I might break a raw egg into it."

- 2 heads garlic, separated into cloves and peeled
- 2 tablespoons olive oil
- 6 cups hot water
- Salt to taste
- Thin slices of French bread
- Optional: 4 eggs and 4 slices of cheese, "cut so thin that the children would hold it up to the light, to admire its transparency, and wink at one another through the frequent round holes"

"Fry the garlic cloves in olive oil in a medium sauce pan until crisp. Remove the larger pieces of garlic. Add hot water, thin slices of bread, and a little salt. Ladle into 4 bowls. If you are feeling rich, break a raw egg into each bowl. Serve, as you can, with more bread and cheese." Serves 4.

"A spade does better in my hand than a Governor's truncheon; and I had rather fill my belly with Gazpacho than lie at the mercy of a coxcombly physick-monger that starves me to death." Miguel de Cervantes (1547-1616) from *Don Quixote*

Gazpacho

Alice B. Toklas (1877-1967), lover of Gertrude Stein, was part of the Paris literary scene along with Hemingway, Fitzgerald, Cowley and others. She wrote her own cookbook in 1954 in which she included her famous marijuana brownie recipe. As she traveled about Spain, she found a great variety of cold gazpacho soups and included a chapter called "Beautiful Soup." This gazpacho from Seville she described as "exquisite."

"In a bowl put 4 crushed cloves of garlic, 1 teaspoon salt, ½ teaspoon powdered Spanish pepper, and the pulp of 2 medium-sized tomatoes, crushed. Mix these ingredients thoroughly and add drop by drop 4 tablespoons olive oil. Add 1 Spanish onion cut in tissue paper thin slices; 1 sweet red or green pepper, seeds removed and cut in minute cubes; 1 cucumber cut in minute cubes; and 4 tablespoons fresh white breadcrumbs. Add 3 cups water; mix thoroughly. Serve ice cold."

"Goodbye good old pork chops
Farewell, beefsteak rare
It's a long way down to the soup line,
But my soup is there."
Union organizer/song writer Joe Hill (1879-1915)

Hamburger Soup

Ronald Reagan, former movie actor, governor and U.S. president, was probably proudest of having been a lifeguard and saving over 80 lives as a young man. His mother held up the model of a religious evangelist to young Ronnie who became a fervent warrior against evil throughout his life.

Ronald Reagan was a writer from an early age. He has a poem in the high school yearbook, his short stories were in high school and college newspapers, he wrote countless newspaper articles, wrote his own speeches, and wrote out his radio addresses on states' rights, abortion, free trade, etc. He wrote his autobiography, *Ronald Reagan.* His writings are in a book called *Reagan In His Own Hand.*

This simple soup portrays the tastes of this humble man, whose handwritten speeches are on view at the Reagan Library. This recipe is available on the Internet.

- 2 pounds lean ground beef
- 2 tablespoons butter
- 2 cups diced onions
- 2 cloves chopped garlic
- 1 ½ cups sliced carrots
- ¼ teaspoon black pepper
- 10 ounces canned hominy

- 1 cup diced green peppers
- 3 quarts beef broth or water with bouillon cubes
- 16 ounces chopped tomato (canned or fresh)
- 2 cups sliced celery

Brown the meat in butter in a large saucepan. Add onions, garlic, carrots, celery and green pepper. Simmer 10 minutes with the pan covered. Add broth/water, add tomato and pepper, and simmer on low for 35 minutes. Add hominy. Boil soup for 10 minutes more. Makes 4 quarts.

"To rise at six, to dine at ten
To sip at six, to sleep at ten
Makes a man live for ten times ten."
Inscription over the study door of Victor Hugo

Les Miserables Soup

Victor Hugo (1802-1885) was the son of an army general. His parents separated when he was a toddler. His mother raised him. Her lover was executed for conspiring to overthrow Napoleon.

In his teens he wrote tragedies, poetry, and translated Virgil. He founded a review wherein he published his poems, inspired by the statesman and author, Francois Chateaubriand. In return, Louis XVIII awarded Hugo a small pension. He wrote plays, poems, and novels, and wrote the story (*Le Roi S'Amuse* or *The King Is Amused*) upon which the opera *Rigoletto* is based. He often wrote about politics in books such as *Cromwell*. He was admitted to political office and took a ten-year hiatus from writing while he tried to promote social justice.

After Napoleon's coup d'etat, he fled to England where he lived 20 years and wrote *Les Miserables* about social justice. In the opening pages, the Bishop serves Jean Valjean a soup with a loaf of rye bread. It consisted of the following ingredients.

- Water
- Oil
- Bread
- Salt
- A little pork
- A scrap of mutton
- A few figs
- Green cheese (aging cheese)

The chances are that a little pork and mutton browned in oil would taste good with some salt and water added. The figs would add a very nice sweetening agent and the thickening might be added by a little cheese. Body would be added by bread, and one might have a soup worthy of a French bistro.

"Many's the long night I've dreamed of cheese—toasted, mostly." Robert Louis Stevenson (1850-1894)

Onion Soup

Vincent Price's (1911-1993) "Soupe a L'Oignon Gratinee" recipe came from his cookbook, *A Treasury of Great Recipes.*

He had written other books before that one. Vincent's dog, Joe, died at the age of 17 in 1964. He decided to write a book about the dog and called it *The Book of Joe: About a Dog and His Man.*

He enjoyed writing so much that he went on to do other works such as *The Michelangelo Bible* in 1964 and *Treasury of Great Recipes* in 1965. This recipe is available on the Internet.

- 3 tablespoons bacon drippings or butter
- 4 large onions, chopped
- 2 tablespoons flour
- ½ teaspoon salt
- 1/8 teaspoon pepper
- 1 garlic clove, minced
- Sprig of parsley
- Pinch of thyme
- 1 quart chicken or beef stock
- 1 cup dry white wine
- 1 tablespoon cognac
- One slice toasted French bread per serving
- Grated Gruyere or Swiss cheese
- Grated Parmesan cheese

In a deep saucepan, heat the drippings or butter. Sauté the onions in the drippings, cooking over medium heat until they are soft. Add the flour, salt, pepper and minced garlic. Cook until the mixture is golden brown but not burned.

Add parsley, thyme, chicken or beef stock, and wine, and simmer for 45 minutes. Add the cognac. Serve in individual ovenproof bowls with one slice toasted French bread in each. Top bread with grated cheese (Gruyere, Swiss, etc.) and top that with grated Parmesan. Place in a very hot oven till cheese melts and forms a brown crust. This serves approximately 6.

"When the ship goes wop with a wiggle between
And the steward falls into the soup tureen..."
Rudyard Kipling (1865-1936)

Puree Mongole Soup

This was F.B.I. Director J. Edgar Hoover's (1895-1972) favorite soup. Hoover, a bachelor, had no wife to cook for him, but was rumored to have had rather interesting parties for his intimates in the F.B.I.

Hoover's father was in the Coast Guard and the Geodetic Survey. His mother was a strong disciplinarian and wanted him to be a minister. He chose to study law after debating in high school to overcome stuttering. He became a clerk in the Justice Department and was soon in charge of Enemy Alien Registration. After serving as Assistant Director of the F.B.I., he became director until his death during the Nixon administration.

Hoover wrote *The Revolution in Action, Masters of Deceit, A Study of Communism* and other works. This recipe is available on the Internet.

- 1 can condensed pea soup
- 1 can condensed tomato soup
- 1 can milk
- 1 can water
- Dash of curry

Mix and heat and serve.

"The time has come," the Walrus said,
"To talk of many things:
Of shoes, and ships, and sealing wax
Of cabbages, and kings."
Lewis Carroll (1832-1898)

Shchi (Russian Cabbage Soup)

Shchi has been a favorite soup of Ivan the Terrible, Nicholas II, Lenin, Stalin, Mao Tse-tung, and Alexander Dumas. Lewis Carroll, author of *Alice in Wonderland,* found it "quite drinkable, though it contained some sour element, which perhaps is necessary for Russian palates." This information and recipe is available on the internet on a wonderful web site entitled Soup Tales.

Russian writer Edouard Limonov wrote in *That's Me, Edichka* about surviving on shchi in New York City: "The advantages of shchi are as follows. There are five of them: 1. It is very cheap, a saucepan of it costs two or three dollars, and it is enough for two days. 2. It doesn't get sour without refrigeration, even when it is very hot. 3. It is cooked quickly, only one and a half hours. 4. It is possible and even necessary to eat it cold. 5. There is no better meal for summer, because it is sour."

- 8-10 dried mushrooms, hydrated in 1 cup hot water 1 hour
- 3 tablespoons butter
- 4 cups shredded cabbage
- 2-3 cups sauerkraut, rinsed with water, squeezed dry
- 2 tablespoons tomato paste
- 12 cups beef or vegetable stock
- 3 tablespoons butter

- 1 carrot, peeled, cut into julienne strips
- 1 ½ cup chopped onion
- 1 stalk celery, diced
- 1 large turnip, peeled and diced
- 1 16 ounce can tomatoes, drained, seeded, chopped
- Salt and pepper
- 1 large clove garlic, minced or pressed
- Chopped fresh dill mixed into sour cream for garnish

Begin by soaking the mushrooms in water. In a large pot, melt 3 tablespoons butter, toss in cabbage and sauerkraut and sauté for 15 minutes, stirring often. Stir in the tomato paste and 1 cup of stock. Cover and simmer on low for 40 minutes.

Squeeze the mushrooms dry and slice finely. Melt the other 3 tablespoons of butter in a skillet and sauté the carrot, onions, celery, turnip, and mushrooms until soft and slightly brown, about 15 minutes.

When the cabbage and kraut are stewed, stir in the sautéed vegetables, the tomatoes and the stock. Season with salt and pepper. Bring to a boil, then cover and simmer on low for 20 minutes. Add garlic and cook 5 more minutes.

Let stand at least 15 minutes or ideally a day or so in the refrigerator to cure. When ready to serve, reheat slowly. Ladle into bowls and garnish with dilled sour cream.

"It was as true… as turnips is. It was as true… as taxes is. And nothing's truer than them." Charles Dickens (1812-1870)

Turnip Soup

Emile Zola wrote about and was associated with the poor people of Paris and the oppressed such as the Jews or the miners. To this day, the turnip soup served in the market section of Paris, Les Halles, is called "Zola's Turnip Soup."

- 2 ¾ cups diced turnips
- 4 cups veal stock
- 1/3 cup raw rice
- ½ cup finely chopped onion
- ¼ to ½ teaspoon curry powder
- 1 tablespoon butter
- Salt and pepper to taste
- 1/3 to ½ cup heavy cream
- Garnish with fried bread cubes

Place diced turnips in a saucepan with boiling veal stock. Cover and bring to a boil. Cook until the turnips are tender. Remove turnips from the stock and put in the rice. Sauté onions and curry in butter until onions are soft and add to the stock.

Cover and cook slowly 15 minutes until the rice is soft. Blend in a food processor. Add salt and pepper, cream and garnish with bread cubes just before serving. Makes 6 servings.

"By this leek, I will most horribly revenge. I eat and eat, I swear." William Shakespeare (1564-1619)

Turtle Soup

Isak Dinesen (1885-1962) was the pen name of Karen Blixen. She wrote *Out of Africa* and *Babette's Feast,* both of which were made into movies. The latter was about a French female chef forced to flee Paris to Norway, where she became something of a female Christ figure.

Although Dinesen did not include recipes for the dishes, those who read the book and saw the movie have created their own versions. This recipe by Teria Gartelos was called "Soupe a la Tortue a las Louisianne" and is modeled after that served in Brennan's in New Orleans. There is an option without turtle at the end of the recipe. This recipe is available on the Internet.

Stock:

- 3 pounds turtle meat
- 3 ½ quarts water
- 2 bay leaves
- 2 teaspoons cayenne pepper
- 2 tablespoons salt
- 2 ribs celery
- 4 cloves garlic
- 1 onion.
- Coriander seed, peppercorns and dried herbs such as basil, marjoram, rosemary and thyme

Soup:
- 1 ½ cups butter
- 2 cups leeks, chopped, white part only
- 1 ½ cups flour
- ½ cup tomato puree
- 1 cup sherry
- ½ cup Worcestershire sauce
- 3 eggs, hardboiled, chopped
- ½ cup parsley, chopped
- Juice of ½ lemon

To make stock, cover the turtle with water and bring to a boil. Skim the foam that rises until the liquid is almost clear. Add the remaining stock ingredients, reduce the heat, cover and simmer at least 2 hours.

Strain and refrigerate the liquid. Remove the turtle meat from the bones; cube and chill the meat. Discard the remaining solids.

To make the soup, melt the butter over low heat and add the leeks. Cook slowly until the leeks are transparent. Whisk in the flour until thick. Add the tomato and cook 5 minutes.

Skim off any fat in the turtle stock and add 10 cups of the stock to the leek mixture, along with the sherry and Worcestershire. Cook 15 minutes. Add the turtle meat and the eggs and simmer 12 more minutes. Stir in the parsley and lemon juice and serve. Makes 15 servings.

Option: To make a vegetarian version without turtle, substitute 2 pounds of chopped button mushrooms and 1 pound chopped Portobello mushrooms for the turtle. Add a chopped apple and pear to the stock.

"He was a bold man that first ate an oyster." Jonathan Swift (1667-1745)

Veal Soup

Alexander Pope (1688-1744) wrote this poetic soup recipe in 1726. He prepared the soup to speed his own recovery from a near fatal accident. He then sent it to his friend, Jonathan Swift, who had recently returned from Ireland. He published it in *Poems on Several Occasions* and called it "Receipt to make Soup: for the Use of Dean Swift."

Pope used some phrases that require explanation. "What's join'd to a place" means celery. "That which Killed King Will" refers to when King William III was killed by his horse named Sorrell (which is a green herb). Thyme (time) "never stands still". The "bed where children are bred" refers to a bed of parsley.

"Take a knuckle of veal (You may buy it, or steal),
In a few pieces cut it, in a stewing pan put it,
Salt, pepper and mace must season this knuckle,
Then what's joined to a place, with other Herbs muckle;
That which killed King Will, and what never stands still,
Some sprigs of that bed where children are bred,
Which much you will mend, if both Spinage and Endive,
And Lettuce and Beet, with Marygold meet;
Put no water at all; for it maketh things small;
Which, lest it should happen, a close cover clap on;
Put this pot of Wood's mettle in a hot boiling kettle,
And there let it be, (Mark the Doctrine I teach)
About... let me see,... Thrice as long as you preach.
So skimming the fat off, say Grace, with your hat off
O then, with what rapture will it fill Dean and Chapter!"

"There's nothing in Christianity or Buddhism that quite matches the sympathetic unselfishness of an oyster." Saki (1870-1916 H. H. Munro)

Veal and Oyster Soup

Vincent Price (1911-1993), movie actor and art connoisseur, wrote a cookbook in 1965 with his wife called *A Treasury of Great Recipes*. He also wrote an article for the *London News* in 1972 called "Re-creating Old London; The American Way of Christmas" which included this recipe, available on the Internet.

- 3 pounds lean veal
- 1 pint cream
- 2 tablespoons cornstarch
- 3 quarts water
- 1 quart oysters

Boil veal slowly in the water until reduced to half the quantity of water. Mash veal in water, strain and cool. Add oysters and all their liquors. Boil for 10 minutes and strain through a cloth. Beat the cream and heat it. Thicken oyster-veal stock with cornstarch, add hot cream, salt and pepper to taste and serve with cold whipped cream on top.

"Do not count your chickens before they are hatched." Aesop (6th century B.C.)

White Soup

Jane Austen (1775-1817) wrote several famous books including *Emma, Sense and Sensibility*, and *Pride and Prejudice*. In the latter work, she referred to "white soup."

There is a recipe for White Soup in *The Jane Austen Cookbook* (by Maria Hubert, published in 1996 by Sutton Publishing,) a compilation of recipes by the wife of Jane's brother. This recipe may have been the one she mentioned, and it is available on the Internet.

- 1 veal knuckle
- 1 medium sized chicken, jointed
- 1 pound lean bacon
- 1 pound white rice
- 6 black peppercorns
- 2 onions, peeled, halved
- 2 cans anchovy fillets
- 3 sprigs each thyme, marjoram, tarragon
- 4 stalks celery, chopped
- 1 cup ground almonds
- 1 egg yolk
- 1 ¼ cup light cream
- Whipped cream and watercress to garnish

Put in large pot veal, chicken, bacon, rice, anchovies, peppercorns, onions, herbs tied in a cloth, celery and add water to cover. Stew until the soup is as strong as you choose it or until the chicken is done. Then strain the stock into a clean pot or bowl. Put it in a cool place and let it stand overnight.

The next day, take off the scum and pour it into a clean pot. Put in the ground almonds. Boil about 10 minutes. Strain it again through a fine sieve or cheesecloth.

Whisk the egg yolk and stir it into the cream. Add this to the cooled soup. Reheat until hot but do not let it boil.

A teaspoon of whipped cream or a few watercress leaves on each bowlful is an optional garnish.

Chapter 5

MAIN DISHES

Roast Beef

"Roast beef, medium, is not only a food; it is a philosophy. Seated at Life's Dining Table, with the menu of Morals before you, your eye wanders a bit over the entrees, the hors d'oeuvres, and the things 'a la' though you know that roast beef, medium, is safe and sane and sure." Edna Ferber (1887-1968)

"If there hadn't been women we'd still be squatting in a cave eating raw meat, because we made civilization in order to impress our girl friends." Orson Welles (1915-1985)

Barry's Chili

Barry Goldwater (1909-1998), former Arizona senator and Republican contender for the presidency, also was an author, photographer, pilot, writer, and ran a bed and breakfast. He wrote *The Conscience of a Conservative, With No Apologies,* and other works.

He submitted this recipe in a chili cook-off contest and it won first prize. Barry was an outdoorsman and once lacking shaving cream on a camping trip, shaved using peanut butter. This recipe is available on the Internet.

- 1 pound coarsely ground beef
- 1 pound dried pinto beans
- 1 can (6 ounces) tomato paste
- 2 cups onions, chopped
- 3 tablespoons hot chili powder
- 1 tablespoon ground cumin
- Salt and water as needed

Soak beans in water, covered, overnight. In a large Dutch oven, cook beef until browned, stirring to make it crumbly. Drain off drippings, if needed.

Add tomato paste, onions and drain beans. Mix chili powder, cumin and season with salt. Stir, bring to a boil, reduce the heat, cover and simmer until the beans are tender (about 5 hours). Serves 4-6.

"One cannot think well, love well, sleep well, if one has not dined well."
Virginia Woolf (1882-1941)

Boeuf au Daube

Virginia Woolf (1882-1941) was one of the early feminists and wrote many short stories, essays, and novels. Some of her best-known works are *Between the Acts, On Being Ill, The Captain's Death Bed, Haunted House* and others.

In her work *To the Lighthouse* she included the following reference to daube of beef, an old French technique in which a rump of beef is cooked very slowly for hours with wine and seasonings.

"Though, in fact, she particularly wished dinner to be nice, with William Bankes dining with them; and to show him she did know how to cook vegetables, she was having vegetables specially done for him, and Boeuf a la au Daube, which had been weighing on Mildred's spirits all day. You stand it in water for twenty four hours; you stir continuously; you add a little bay leaf and then a dash of sherry; the whole never being allowed, of course, to come to the boil. It did not matter how late they were."

"I am falser than vows made in wine." William Shakespeare (1564-1619)

Cacciatore

Sophia Loren, primarily known for her movies, has written *Women and Beauty* and *In the Kitchen With Love.* In the latter, she says that it is the sweet red peppers that make chicken cacciatore really Neapolitan. This recipe is available on the Internet.

- 3 tablespoons extra-virgin olive oil
- 8 serving pieces of chicken
- 1 medium onion, sliced
- 1 sweet red pepper, cut in small strips
- ½ cup dry white wine
- ¾ teaspoon salt
- Pinch hot red pepper flakes
- 2 cups canned tomatoes, drained, chopped
- 1/3 cup fresh torn or cut basil

In a large sauté pan with a cover, heat the oil and brown the chicken on the skin side first, then the underside. Do not crowd the pan. Brown it in batches if necessary, setting aside the browned chicken until the rest is done.

When the last of the chicken is almost browned and still in the pan, add the onion and red pepper and sauté until tender.

Arrange the browned chicken in the pan, skin side up, and add the white wine. Season with salt and red pepper flakes, then let the wine cook until it has almost entirely evaporated, just a couple of minutes. While it is reducing, turn the chicken in the liquid once or twice, but leave it skin side up at the end.

Add the tomatoes. Cover the pan, lower the heat, and let it cook at a gentle simmer for about 30 minutes or until the chicken is done.

Remove the chicken to a service platter, increase the heat to high and let the sauce reduce for about two minutes. Add the basil, simmer a few seconds, then pour the sauce over the chicken and serve immediately. Serves 4.

"The carp was killed, assassinated, murdered in the first, second and third degree. Limp, I fell into a chair with my hands still unwashed, reached for a cigarette, lighted it and waited for the police to come and take me into custody." Alice B. Toklas (1877-1967)

Carp

Adlai Stevenson (1900-1965) ran for and lost the presidency and was ambassador to the United Nations under President John F. Kennedy. He wrote speeches and books which John Steinbeck described as far better than anything other politicians wrote with the exception of Abraham Lincoln.

His works are *What I Think, Friends and Enemies, The Citizen and His Government, Continuing Education and the Unfinished Business of American Society, Toward a New America, Ambassador to the United Nations, Why Not Victory?, The Adlai E. Stevenson Memorial Lectures,* and others.

His wife wrote a cookbook which was called *Adlai's Nancy—Her Potpourri* which featured two of Adlai's favorites: Quiche Lorraine and Crown Roast with Cranberry Stuffing. Adlai had his own unique contribution to cuisine.

"Take a 1-2 pound carp, and allow it to swim in clear water for 24 hours. Kill the carp, then scale and fillet it. Rub the fillets with butter and season them with salt and pepper. Place on a board and bake in a moderate oven for 20 minutes. Then throw away the carp and eat the board."

"The cow is of the bovine ilk;
One end is moo, the other, milk."
Ogden Nash (1902-1971)

Catfish in Cajun Cream Sauce

John Grisham grew up in Jonesboro, Arkansas, but moved to Mississippi for his schooling. He graduated from Mississippi State University and earned his law degree from the University of Mississippi. He practiced criminal and civil law, and was elected to the Mississippi House of Representatives.

After the success of his first novels, *A Time To Kill* and *The Firm*, he resigned from the House of Representatives. He later wrote *The Pelican Brief, The Client, The Chamber, The Rainmaker, The Testament, The Brethren,* and *Skipping Christmas,* many of which have been made into movies.

He took over publishing the floundering Oxford American magazine and revived it by running *A Painted House* serially in the magazine. He has written the screenplay for *Mickey,* which is currently being made into a movie.

He loves catfish and said of this recipe, "Pan-fried catfish in a Cajun cream sauce is my favorite."

- 2 eggs
- 1 cup milk
- 2 cups all-purpose flour
- 1 ¼ teaspoons salt, divided
- 1 ½ teaspoons ground red pepper, divided
- 4 6-ounce catfish fillets
- Vegetable oil

- 12 unpeeled, large fresh shrimp
- 1 tablespoon butter or margarine
- 2 teaspoons minced garlic
- ¼ cup white vermouth
- 2 cups whipping cream
- ¼ cup chopped green onions, divided
- 2 teaspoons lemon juice
- 3 slices thinly sliced cooked ham
- Lemon wedges for garnish

Stir the eggs and milk together. Combine the flour, 1 teaspoon of salt and ½ teaspoon of ground red pepper in a shallow dish. Dredge fillets in flour mixture; dip in milk mixture, and dredge again in flour mixture. Pour oil to a depth of 3 inches in a Dutch oven; heat to 360 degrees. Fry the fillets 6 minutes or until golden; drain on paper towels. Keep warm.

Peel shrimp. Melt butter in a large skillet over medium heat. Add shrimp and garlic and cook, stirring often, 3 to 5 minutes or until shrimp turn pink. Remove shrimp, and set aside, reserving drippings in the skillet.

Stir vermouth into reserved drippings; bring to a boil and cook 1 minute. Add whipping cream, 2 tablespoons green onions, lemon juice, remaining ¼ teaspoon salt, and remaining red pepper. Cook, stirring often, 12 to 15 minutes or until sauce is thickened.

Arrange catfish on a serving plate, and drizzle with sauce. Top with shrimp and julienned ham strips; sprinkle with remaining 2 tablespoons chopped green onions. Garnish with lemon wedges.

"I rather like bad wine. One gets so bored with good wine." Benjamin Disraeli (1804-1881)

Chicken a la Creole

Cajun entertainer and chef Justin Wilson (1914-2001) wrote several cook books including *Outside Cooking With Inside Help, Justin Wilson's Easy Cooking, Justin Wilson Looking Back, Justin Wilson Homegrown Louisiana Cookin', Justin Wilson Cajun Humor, Justin Wilson's Cajun Fables, More Cajun Humor,* and other works.

About this dish, he said, "Dis is a delightful dish. It is so easy to fix, I garontee!" This recipe is available on the Internet.

- ¼ cup dried onion
- 1 tablespoon dried green onions
- 1 tablespoon dried parsley
- 1 teaspoon garlic powder
- 4 cups water or chicken stock
- 1 cup dry white wine
- 1 cup Rotel spiced tomatoes
- 3 tablespoons steak sauce
- 1-2 teaspoons Louisiana hot sauce or ½ tsp. cayenne pepper
- 4 cups canned peeled tomatoes
- 4 cups boneless boiled chicken pieces
- 1 teaspoon dried mint

Mix the onions, green onions, parsley and garlic powder with 2 cups of water/stock and set aside for about 1 hour.

Meanwhile combine the remaining 2 cups water/stock with the wine, tomatoes, steak sauce, hot sauce/cayenne and tomatoes in a large pot and cook for about 30 minutes over a low fire.

Combine all, heat, and serve.

"I want there to be no peasant in my realm so poor that he will not have a chicken in his pot every Sunday." Henry IV, known as Henry of Navarre (1553-1610)

Chicken and Dumplings

Rex Stout (1886-1975) wrote many Nero Wolfe mysteries as well as *The Nero Wolfe Cookbook*. This recipe is available on the Internet and in the cookbook and is called "Nero Wolfe's Fritz's Chicken Fricassee with Dumplings." Nero's cook was Fritz and his "gofer" was Archie. Archie described the scene in which this recipe was mentioned.

"Lily said, 'The fricassee with dumplings is made by a Mrs. Miller whose husband has left her four times on account of her disposition and returned four times on account of her cooking and is still there.'

"We babbled on. The fricassee came, and the first bite, together with dumplings and gravy, made me marvel at the hellishness of Mrs. Miller's disposition to drive a man away from that."

Chicken:
- 4-5 pound chicken
- 1 celery stalk, sliced
- 1 small onion, sliced
- 1 small carrot, sliced

- 6 black peppercorns
- 1 bay leaf
- 1 teaspoon salt
- 3 tablespoons butter
- 3 tablespoons all-purpose flour
- ½ cup heavy cream
- 1 egg yolk
- 1 teaspoon lemon juice

Cut the chicken into serving pieces and place them in a large pot. Add the celery, onion and carrot to the chicken with the peppercorns and bay leaf. Cover with cold water. Bring to a boil, cover and simmer until the chicken is tender, about 1 hour. Add the salt.

Melt the butter in a saucepan and add the flour. Cook for 3 minutes and gradually pour in 2 cups of the strained chicken stock, stirring constantly until the sauce is thickened.

Blend the cream and egg yolk and add to the sauce. Heat thoroughly and season with lemon juice and more salt if needed.

Arrange the chicken pieces on a warm platter and pour the sauce over. Serves 4.

Dumplings:
- ½ pound fresh spinach
- 1 cup ricotta cheese
- ½ cup + 2 tablespoons grated Parmesan cheese
- 1 teaspoon salt
- ¼ teaspoon fresh ground black pepper
- 1 large egg
- 3 tablespoons melted butter
- ½ cup all-purpose flour
- 2 cups chicken stock

Wash, trim, and blanch the spinach in salt water. Drain well and chop fine. Mix well with the cheeses (except 2 tablespoons of Parmesan) salt, pepper, egg and half the butter. Refrigerate for 1 hour.

Shape the dough into balls; roll them in flour and drop, a few at a time, into gently boiling chicken stock. As soon as they rise to the surface, remove with a slotted spoon to a hot buttered baking dish.

Preheat the broiler. Sprinkle the dumplings with the additional Parmesan cheese, drizzle with the melted butter and broil until a hot flame occurs and the cheese browns. Makes 12 dumplings for 4 servings of 3 each.

"Temptations can be got rid of." "How?" "By yielding to them." Honore de Balzac

Chicken Breast Berlioz

It was difficult to know which person to associate with this recipe. The recipe was dedicated to Hector Berlioz who passed time in cafes and restaurants in between writing famous music and operas (*Benvenuto Cellini* and *Beatrice and Benedict* for example). Berlioz wrote his memoirs, his journal of literary critiques and composed his oratorio, *The Childhood of Christ* while in restaurants.

This recipe was served to Berlioz and Honore de Balzac on October 12, 1838, when they came to the Café de Paris to celebrate the opening of Berlioz' *Benvenuto Cellini.*

Balzac (1799-1850) wrote *Cezar Birotteau, The Chouans, The Country Doctor, Counsin Pette, Engenie Grandet, Father Goriot, Lost Illusions, The Wild Ass's Skin*, and many other works.

Chicken:
- 4 chicken breasts, halved
- Salt and pepper to taste
- 2 eggs, beaten with 2 teaspoons water
- ¼ cup flour
- ¼ cup butter
- 1 cup chicken stock
- 1 cup cream
- Juice of 1 lemon

Artichoke Hearts:
- 1 ½ cups mushrooms, chopped
- 2 tablespoons butter
- 2 tablespoons cream
- 2 tablespoons onion, chopped
- Salt and pepper to taste
- 8 large or 16 small artichoke hearts, cooked, at room temperature (can be frozen but not canned)

Chicken:

Sprinkle the chicken with salt and pepper. Dip each half first in the beaten egg mixture and then in the flour to coat lightly.

In a skillet melt the butter and sauté the breasts for about 5 minutes, turning once or twice. Add the stock and cream, just bring to a boil and reduce the fire to a gentle simmer for 10 minutes.

Remove from heat and set aside to keep warm.

Artichokes:

While the chicken is cooking, prepare the artichoke hearts. In a skillet melt the butter and sauté the onions and mushrooms until they are brown. Add the cream and salt and pepper and heat through.

With this mixture fill the artichoke hearts and place in an oven that has been preheated to 200 degrees for 5 minutes.

To serve, place the chicken breasts on a warm serving plate, and pour over the sauce. Surround the chicken breasts with the artichoke hearts and serve piping hot.

"Tongue; well, that's a very good thing when it ain't a woman's. Charles Dickens (1812-1870)

Chicken Fricassee

In 1819 Thomas Jefferson (1743-1826) wrote, "I lived temperately, eating little animal food." He loved vegetables and his garden contained virtually every imaginable vegetable.

His Monticello cookbook contained a recipe for cabbage leaves filled with pigs' tongues and boiled carrots to be cooked for two hours.

In case that recipe doesn't sound particularly palatable, this chicken dish will be found quite tasty. This recipe is available on the Internet.

- 2-3 pounds chicken pieces
- 1 teaspoon salt
- ½ teaspoon ground nutmeg
- ½ teaspoon pepper
- ½ teaspoon paprika
- 3 tablespoons all purpose flour
- 2 cups water
- 1 cup dry white wine
- 3 tablespoons butter

- 1 onion, chopped
- 2 cups fresh small mushrooms
- 1 tablespoon chopped fresh sage
- 1 tablespoon chopped fresh parsley
- 1 cup half and half cream
- Hot cooked rice

Wash and dry chicken pieces and season with salt, pepper, nutmeg and paprika. Brown the chicken in hot oil over high heat until browned. Remove the chicken. Reduce heat, add flour and cook until lightly browned, stirring constantly. Whisk in 2 cups water, 1 cup wine and stir until smooth. Return the chicken to the pan, bring to a boil, cover and reduce heat. Cook 50 minutes.

Remove chicken, keeping warm, reserve the broth in a large container. Remove large particles.

Melt butter in another pan, add onion and cook until light golden. Add mushrooms, sage and parsley. Add broth and chicken. Cook until thoroughly heated. Serve over rice. Serves 6.

"Mankind possesses two supreme blessings. First of these is the goddess Demeter. It was she who gave to man his nourishment of grain. But after her there came the son of Semele, who matched her present by inventing liquid wine as his gift to man. For filled with that good gift, suffering mankind forgets its grief; from it comes sleep; with it oblivion of the troubles of the day. There is no other medicine for misery." Euripides (480-406 B.C.)

Chicken in Champagne Sauce

Vincent Price (1911-1993) may become better known for his incredible gourmet and cuisine tastes than for his acting as time goes by. The

Internet is filled with compliments of the recipes in the cookbooks that he wrote with his wife, Mary. The two of them picked up recipes from famous restaurants across the world. This recipe has achieved a Nirvana status among those who have made the dish.

- 3-pound chicken
- 1 teaspoon salt
- 2 tablespoons butter
- 2 cups dry French champagne
- 4 cups cream
- 3 shallots, chopped fine
- 4 mushrooms, crushed by rolling pin
- 1 sprig parsley, chopped
- 2 bay leaves
- A pinch of thyme
- 2 tablespoons butter
- 6 ounces dry French champagne

Preheat the oven to 350 degrees. Season the chicken with salt. Truss it and place it in a small casserole with 2 tablespoons butter and 2 cups champagne. Cook in the oven for 45 minutes. Baste every 8 minutes and turn until the chicken is an even gold brown on all sides. Remove the chicken, cut off the string, and keep it warm on a hot platter.

To make the sauce, add the cream shallots, mushrooms, parsley, bay leaves and thyme to the juices in the casserole. Simmer on the stove until reduced to 2/3 of the original amount. Strain through a fine sieve into a clean saucepan. Place over medium heat and swirl in 2 tablespoons butter and 6 ounces champagne.

To serve, spoon some of the sauce over the chicken and serve the rest of the sauce separately. At the Pavillon Restaurant in New York where Vincent and Mary had this dish, the chicken was brought to the table whole and carved there by the captain.

"Man and the animals are merely a passage and channel for food, a tomb for other animals." Leonardo da Vinci (1452-1519)

Chicken Sweet and Hot

Vincent Price (1911-1993), actor, art connoisseur, and chef, wrote several cookbooks and food articles for magazines.

He was also a frequent guest on television. He was a very big hit on the television quiz show *The $64,000 Question*, where he displayed his knowledge of art. He liked serving dishes that surprised people, which included this one. This recipe is available on the Internet.

- 1 chicken, quartered
- ½ cup butter
- ¼ cup Worcestershire sauce
- 1 large clove garlic, minced
- ½ cup red currant jelly
- 1 tablespoon Dijon mustard
- 1 cup orange juice
- 1 teaspoon powdered ginger
- 3 dashes Tabasco sauce

Combine all of the ingredients except the chicken in a pan. Heat gently for 15-20 minutes. Cool. Pour the sauce over the quartered chicken and marinate for 2 to 3 hours. Then cover and cook at 350 for 45 minutes. Uncover, increase oven temperature to hot, baste chicken frequently, and cook until chicken is dark brown.

Serve with rice. Serves 4.

"Americans can eat garbage, provided you sprinkle it liberally with ketchup, mustard, chili sauce, Tabasco sauce, cayenne pepper, or any other condiment which destroys the original flavor of the dish." Henry Miller (1891-1980)

Chili and Beans

Cartoonist and writer Walt Disney contributed this recipe to the *Walt Disney Cookbook* produced by his staff.

- 2 pounds dried pinto beans
- 2 medium onions, sliced
- ¼ cup vegetable oil
- 2 cloves garlic, diced
- 1 piece celery, chopped
- 2 pounds ground beef
- 1 teaspoon chili powder, or more
- 1 teaspoon paprika
- 1 teaspoon dried thyme
- 28 ounce can tomatoes
- Salt and pepper
- Options for spicier version:

- 1/8 teaspoon coriander
- 1/8 teaspoon turmeric
- 1/8 teaspoon chili seeds
- 1/8 teaspoon fennel
- 1/8 teaspoon cloves
- 1/8 teaspoon cinnamon
- 1/8 teaspoon dried ginger
- 1 small Mexican chili pepper

Wash, sort and soak beans in cold water overnight. Drain; place in 2 quart saucepan. Add water to cover 2" over beans.

The next morning, add onions and simmer in covered pot until tender, 2 hours. Meanwhile, heat oil in large saucepan; sauté garlic until lightly browned. Add celery and beef; cook. Add chili powder, paprika, and thyme. Break up tomatoes with spoon and mix with meat mixture; cover, simmer 1 hour.

When beans are tender, combine with meat, stirring gently. Salt and pepper and add additional spices if desired, and cook 30 more minutes.

"A man must take the fat with the lean." Charles Dickens (1812-1870)

Chinese Chicken

Vincent Price (1911-1993) had impeccable taste in cuisine. Although he usually included recipes in his cookbook of European origin, here is an exception. He once wrote cleverly, "If chicken always tastes better in a Chinese restaurant, it's not just an occident."

Here is his recipe, written while he was a spokesman for Angostura aromatic bitters. He didn't always give exact measurements, expecting the cook to supply these to taste. This recipe is available on the Internet in an ad for Angostura Bitters.

- 6 chicken fryer halves
- Salt
- Garlic powder
- 3 cups tomato sauce
- 1 cup pineapple juice
- 1 tablespoon Angostura bitters
- 1 tablespoon grated onion
- ½ cup melted butter or margarine.

Sprinkle fryers with salt and garlic powder. Then in a saucepan combine tomato sauce, juice, bitters, onion and butter or margarine. Simmer until the mixture boils.

Brush on chicken. Bake in a 350 degree oven for one hour, brushing several times with the liquid.

"I don't take notes; I don't outline, I don't do anything like that. I just flail away at the goddamned thing. I'm a salami writer. I try to write good salami, but salami is salami. You can't sell it as caviar." Stephen King

Cincinnati Chili

Betty Stoneking began writing after her father's death. She said, "It began to flow like a journal of my struggle to find myself."

She founded a real estate appraisal school in Arizona and wrote course material for it.

She wrote *America's Phoenix Generation: Heroes of World War II* in 1998 about reunions of veterans of the "greatest generation." Her web site is www.sun-city-west-az.com/center.

She said, "Cincinnati is famous for their chili dishes served over hot spaghetti, topped with shredded cheddar cheese, onions and oyster crackers. There is one famous chili outlet with an added secret ingredient that gives their chili that mysterious irresistible hot and sweet flavor at the same time and brings you back time and again. Want to know what it is? Chocolate!

Try adding 2-3 tablespoons of Ghirardelli double chocolate hot chocolate powder to the pot. I'll bet you'll love the undertone tangy flavor that no one can figure out."

- 2 pounds ground beef
- 4 medium onions chopped
- 1 clove garlic minced
- 2 teaspoons vinegar or burgundy wine
- 1 can (12 ounces) tomato paste
- 2-3 teaspoons chili powder
- 3 teaspoons cinnamon
- 1 teaspoon Tabasco
- 2 dashes Worcestershire sauce
- 1 quart water
- Salt and pepper
- Spice bag (4 dry peppers, 35 allspice kernels, 5 bay leaves)

Sauté beef, onions, and garlic. Add all other ingredients and simmer, partially covered, one hour. Remove the spice bag. Serve over spaghetti with cheese, onions and crackers on the side. Serves 6 to 8.

"You've got to sell your heart, your strongest reactions, not the little minor things that only touch you lightly, the little experiences that you might tell at dinner. This is especially true when you begin to write, when you have not yet developed the tricks of interesting people on paper." F. Scott Fitzgerald (1896-1940)

Clam and Eggs

Rex Stout's (1886-1975) mysteries featured many unusual dishes eaten by his gourmand sleuth, Nero Wolfe. This recipe is in Stout's *Nero Wolfe's Cookbook* and is called "Clams Hashed with Eggs."

- 2 dozen cherrystone clams
- 3 tablespoons butter
- 6 large mushrooms
- 1 large green pepper
- 4 large eggs
- 2 pounds potatoes
- 1 tablespoon fresh parsley, chopped
- 1 tablespoon fresh chives, chopped
- 2 teaspoons salt
- ¼ teaspoon ground black pepper
- 1 tablespoon dry sherry
- ¼ teaspoon paprika
- 6 slices bacon

Preheat the oven to 350 degrees. Shuck and mince the clams. Sauté them in butter for 5 minutes. Slice the mushrooms and chop the green pepper and add them to the pan, cooking until they begin to brown. Remove the clams and vegetables from the heat and drain.

Beat the eggs. Boil the unpeeled potatoes until tender in salted water. Remove the skins and slice. Combine the eggs and potatoes in a large bowl with the parsley, chives, salt, pepper and sherry. Mix well. Fold in the clams, green pepper and mushrooms. Pour the mixture into a well-buttered baking dish.

Sprinkle with paprika and bake for 30-35 minutes. Meanwhile, cook the bacon strips until they are crisp. Drain and crumble the bacon and garnish the finished casserole before serving. Serves 4.

"Pepper is small in quantity and great in virtue." Plato

Cod Casserole

Rex Stout (1886-1975) described this dish in his Nero Wolfe mystery, *Prisoner's Base.* He included the recipe in his *Nero Wolfe Cookbook.* Quite a food connoisseur, he called it Portuguese Salt Cod and based it on a Portuguese recipe called Bacalhau.

- 1 ½-2 pounds soaked dried cod*
- 2 large onions, sliced
- 6 tablespoons butter
- 1 clove garlic, minced
- 3 large potatoes
- 2 tablespoons bread crumbs
- 10 pitted green olives
- 10 black olives
- 4 hard-cooked eggs
- ½ cup chopped fresh parsley

- Wine vinegar
- Olive oil
- Lots of freshly ground black pepper

*Note: To prepare dried cod, soak in cold water for about 24 hours, or until it is completely moistened. Change the water two or three times. Drain thoroughly.

Put the cod in a saucepan and add enough cold water to cover. Bring to a boil, reduce the heat, and simmer for 15 minutes, or until the fish is tender. Drain, remove the skin and bones. Flake the meat with a fork into large pieces.

Sauté the onions in 3 tablespoons butter until they are tender and golden in color. Add the garlic. Boil the unpeeled potatoes in salted water. When they are tender, remove from the heat, put under cold running water, and remove the skins. Drain and slice into ¼ inch pieces.

Preheat the oven to 350 degrees. Grease a 1 ½ quart casserole with the remaining 3 tablespoons of butter. Arrange a layer of half the potatoes, then half the cod, then half the onions. Sprinkle with a little pepper and repeat the layering. Sprinkle the bread crumbs over the top layer.

Bake for 15 minutes, or until heated through and lightly browned. Before serving, garnish the top with olives and eggs; sprinkle with parsley. Serve with the wine vinegar and oil in cruets and black pepper in a small dish.

"A writer is like a bean plant; he has his little day and then gets stringy." E. B. White (1899-1985)

Corn and Bean Chili

Poet and short story writer, Lydia Boyer, professes not to be a cook. But nobody can believe that after sampling this dish. Originally, she was a company and customer instructor and writer for AT&T.

She is the Poet Laureate of RISE, likes editing, dialogue and short stories. Two of her poems have been prizewinners. Lydia was the former editor of the Arizona Poetry Society Journal, *Sandcutter.*

- 1 lb. ground beef
- 1 medium onion, chopped
- 1 envelope Hidden Valley original ranch seasoning
- 1 envelope taco seasoning
- 1 14-ounce can of beans (pinto, kidney, or red) undrained
- 1 can whole corn, undrained
- 1 can stewed tomatoes, undrained
- ½ cup water or tomato juice
- 2 teaspoons vinegar
- ¼ teaspoon sugar.

In a large skillet, brown the meat and onion
Drain it so it won't be greasy.
Open all the envelopes and cans.
Then add and stir them in; it's easy!
Quickly add the canned food too,
Mix and boil for just a few.
Cover and turn the heat down low.

Simmer and let it cook real slow.
After half an hour or more,
This can serve three folks or four.

"Fish and visitors smell in three days." Benjamin Franklin (1706-1790)

Dishwasher Fish

Vincent (1911-1993) and Mary Price wrote *A Treasury of Great Recipes* in 1965 and *Mary and Vincent Price's Come into the Kitchen Cookbook* in 1970. In 1965, Vincent was named International Ambassador for California Wines. He threw a gala evening in honor of this appointment. Among the movie stars and friends invited was Ronald Reagan.

Vincent introduced a dish that "any fool can prepare" on the Johnny Carson *Tonight Show* on November 21, 1975. He prepared steamed fish in a Westinghouse dishwasher. For years thereafter, he was asked for this recipe.

- 1 fish
- Salt and pepper
- Juice of 1 lemon
- 1 lemon thinly sliced

Season the fish lightly with salt, pepper and lemon juice. Place lemon slices on both outer sides of the fish and wrap the fish in aluminum foil. Place it in a dishwasher without soap or dishes, and steam it by running it on the regular cycle.

"Fame is the thirst of youth." George Gordon, Lord Byron (1788-1824)

Dolmades

British pop singer Cat Stevens, best known for his composition *Morning Has Broken,* was a multi-talented artist, cook, and UNESCO helper. He gave up his career in 1978 to open a school for Muslim children in London, after converting to the Islamic faith and taking the new name Yusuf Islam. He created a children's book that also became an animated cartoon called *Teaser and the Firecat.* This recipe is available on the Internet.

- Vine leaves (from Greek food shops)
- ½ pound mincemeat, cooked
- ¼ cup rice, cooked
- 1 onion, chopped
- 1 teaspoon each chopped parsley and mint
- 1 egg, beaten
- Seasoning to taste
- 2 lemons
- 1 small can tomatoes
- 1 tablespoon tomato puree
- ¼ pint good stock

Boil the vine leaves in salted water and set aside to drain. Bind the mincemeat, rice, onion, parsley, mint, egg and seasonings together and place a small portion on each of the vine leaves. Roll each leaf around the mixture and secure the parcels with a cocktail stick. Place the bundle in a buttered oven dish.

Squeeze juice of 1 lemon over the dolmades. Chop the tomatoes, mix with the tomato puree, stock and season to taste. Pour the sauce over the dolmades. Cover and cook at 350 degrees for 30 minutes. Serve with a generous wedge of lemon. May be served hot or cold.

"It's a naïve domestic Burgundy without any breeding, but I think you'll be amused by its presumption." James Thurber (1894-1961)

Duck

Vincent Price (1911-1993), movie actor, chef, author, and artist came from a wealthy family with a food background. His father was a prominent candy manufacturer and his grandfather invented baking powder. He intended to make a career in art, and earned a bachelor's degree in art from Yale and a master's degree in art from the famous London School of Art. After teaching school for one year, he tried his hand at acting and won his first role because of his facility with chewing gum.

He and his second wife wrote a cookbook from which this recipe is taken. Chef Frederic of the premiere restaurant of Paris, *Tour d'Argent*, personally gave it to the Prices. It was called "Pressed Duck with Duck Blood and Liver Sauce." This recipe is available on the Internet.

- Duck
- 1 cup Port
- 2/3 cup Madeira
- Juice of 1 lemon
- Salt and pepper
- ½ cup Cognac

Make about ½ cup of consommé of a duck. The liver of the duck should be crushed and saved in a bowl. Roast the duck about 15 minutes. Put the crushed liver in a dish with port, Madeira, and cognac. Slice the duck in small pieces. (Duck legs should be broiled for a second course.)

Crush the bones in a "Press Duck" machine or with mortar and pestle to extract blood. Pour in about 1/3 cup consommé of duck to the blood. Pour the juice into the liver/liquor mixture. Cook in a saucepan until thick and similar to the color of melted chocolate. Add salt and pepper to taste.

Beat the sauce "without interruption for 20 minutes."

Heat and serve the sauce over heated duck pieces and/or duck legs but allow the duck pieces to be warm but as rare as possible.

"A man will be eloquent if you give him good wine." Ralph Waldo Emerson (1803-1882)

Eggs with Sherry

This unique recipe for eggs was attributed to Rex Stout (1889-1975) who wrote Nero Wolfe stories, according to an article in *The Washington Post* on February 24, 1972. The recipe was entitled "Eggs Nero Wolfe," when it was included in John Garavelli's *An Eclectic Cookbook.* This recipe is available on the Internet.

- 1 tablespoon butter
- 2 eggs
- 1 tablespoon dry sherry

In a small skillet with a tight fitting cover, melt the butter over high heat until it begins to brown. Fry the eggs lowering the heat to medium, and when the whites begin to set, add the sherry to the skillet. Cover and cook for one to two minutes, allowing the steam to cook the tops of the eggs.

Pour the liquid remaining in the skillet over the eggs when they are served. Rum or bourbon can be substituted for the sherry.

"The shelf life of the modern hardback writer is somewhere between the milk and the yogurt." Calvin Trillin

Fifteen Minute Eggs

Polish entertainer and pianist Liberace (1919-1987) wrote a cookbook called *Liberace Cooks.* He vetoed the original humorous title, "Mother, I'd Rather Do It Myself." A bachelor, he wrote this breakfast recipe for one, called "Special 15 minute Eggs." This recipe is available on the internet.

- 1 tablespoon butter
- 2 eggs
- ½ cup half and half or light cream
- ¼ teaspoon salt
- 1/8 teaspoon pepper
- 2 teaspoons grated Parmesan cheese

Warm a baking dish about 2 ½ to 3 inches across. Put in a little butter. Then break in the eggs. Pour over the half and half/cream, which should almost cover the eggs. Dot with the remaining butter. Sprinkle with salt, pepper and cheese. Bake in a preheated 375 degree oven for 7 to 8 minutes until the whites are set.

"Reading maketh a full man, conference a ready man, and writing an exact man." Francis Bacon (1561-1626)

Finnan Haddie

This dish was mentioned in Rex Stout's (1886-1975) *The Mother Hunt*, another one of his Nero Wolfe mysteries. Finnan Haddie is a Scottish term for smoked haddock. The recipe is in Stout's book, *The Nero Wolfe Cookbook*. This recipe is available on the Internet.

- 2 pounds (smoked haddock)
- 1 cup milk
- 1 cup water
- ¼ cup butter
- 3 tablespoons flour
- 2 cups heavy cream
- Black pepper to taste
- 1/8 teaspoon nutmeg
- 1 tablespoon chopped pimiento
- 4 hard cooked eggs
- Bread crumbs
- 12 bread triangles fried in anchovy butter*

*See Appetizer: Bread Fried in Anchovy Butter

Soak haddock in water to cover for 1 hour. Drain and put in a large saucepan, covering with the milk and water. Bring to a boil, remove from the heat and let stand for 10 to 15 minutes. When cooled, remove the skin and bones, reserving the stock.

Melt the butter in a heavy-bottomed saucepan. Stir in the flour and cook over direct low heat until smooth. Add the cream and 1 ¼ cups of the reserved stock; continue to cook, stirring occasionally, until the mixture is slightly thickened. Season with pepper and nutmeg. When the sauce is thick enough to coat a spoon, remove it from the heat, measure out ¼ cup, and set it aside.

Break the haddock into pieces and fold them into the sauce. Simmer gently over low heat for a few minutes until the fish is warmed.

Pour the mixture into a shallow casserole; cover with the pimiento and sliced hard-cooked eggs and pour the reserved ¼ cup of sauce over the eggs. Sprinkle the dish with breadcrumbs and place under a hot broiler to brown. Serve with the anchovy toast. Serves 4.

"Ruling a big country is like cooking a small fish. Too much handling will spoil it." Lao Tsu (400 B.C.)

Fish Platter

Marcel Proust (1871-1922) who is best known for *Remembrance of Things Past* often wrote about food fondly, and especially French food. He tended to favor elaborate meals and exquisite tastes. He wrote of a fish platter. It included the following arranged on a large platter and accompanied by chilled champagne and white wine.

- Smoked salmon
- Sturgeon
- Whitefish
- Eel
- Two types of herring
- Tuna
- Thinly sliced rye bread
- Sweet butter
- Thinly sliced onions
- Capers
- Thinly sliced cucumbers with oil, vinegar, dill

"Some books are to be tasted, others to be swallowed, and some few to be chewed and digested; that is, some books are to be read only in parts, others to be read, but not curiously; and some few to be read wholly and with diligence and attention." Francis Bacon (1561-1626)

Forfar Bridies

Pasties and meat pies are traditional English fare but the Scottish have their version of these. Sir J. M. Barrie (1860-1937) wrote *Peter Pan, The Admirable Crichton* and many other works. He may have been inspired to write about the boy who wouldn't grow up because he adopted five boys.

Barrie lived in a Scottish town called Forfar in Angus. He referred to the little pies in one of his works, *Sentimental Tommy* as "Forfar bridies." This is the modern version of the traditional recipe for that dish. This recipe is available on the Internet.

- 1 pound chuck steak
- 2/3 cup shredded suet OR
- 2 tablespoons butter and ¼ cup stock
- 1 finely chopped onion
- 1 teaspoon mustard powder
- 4 cups plain flour
- Pinch of salt
- ½ cup margarine and ½ cup shortening

Make the pastry by sifting the flour and salt together, and add the shortenings with a pastry blender. (The shortenings used to be lard in the past.) Stir in enough cold water to make a stiff dough and then turn onto a floured surface; knead gently. Divide the dough into four pieces.

Trim the fat from steak, then tenderize it by pounding. Cut the meat into thin strips (about fajita size) and mix with suet (or butter and stock,) and onion and plenty of seasoning. Roll each piece of dough out to a 6 inch round shape. Divide the filling among each piece of dough and seal the edges well with water.

Make a hole in the center of each bridie, and bake at 400 degrees for 20 minutes. Turn down the temperature to 350 degrees and bake 35 to 40 more minutes or until golden brown. Serve hot. These are often served with peas and potatoes.

"Great chieftan o' the puddin' race!" Robert Burns (1759-1796)

Haggis

Robert Burns (1759-1796) wrote Scottish poems and songs in the Scottish dialect. The freshest leanest haggis is traditionally served the week before his birthday (January 25th) because he wrote so glowingly about the dish. Not only is the dish very strange, but the container for the dish makes it nearly impossible to obtain.

As if that were not enough, the ceremony used in presenting the haggis is formidable. A bit of this can perhaps be conveyed by this recipe. This recipe is available on the Internet.

- 1 pound lean lamb
- 4 onions
- Salt and pepper
- Sheep stomach
- 2 cups oatmeal
- 4 ounces ground suet
- Lamb pluck (heart, liver and lungs)

Wash the stomach bag thoroughly in salted water. Boil the pluck (the heart is considered the seat of courage in an animal) for 1 ½ hours leaving the windpipe attached and hanging out of the pot into another dish. This allows the "impurities" to pass out of it.

When cooked and cold, cut away windpipe and gristle and any skin. Reserve some of the lungs, mince the heart and liver with the lamb meat and chop.

Add suet. Toast oatmeal in the oven and chop onions. Savory herbs may be added if desired.

In a large bowl, mix the minced ingredients, oatmeal, onions, herbs, pepper and salt with about a pint of the stock in which the pluck was boiled. Mix to soft consistency.

Take the stomach bag and spoon the mixture in until rather more than half filled. This allows for the meal to expand. Sew up firmly and prick thoroughly. Tie in a cloth. Place in a pan of boiling water with a plate in the bottom and boil for 3 or 4 hours. Prick occasionally to prevent bursting.

Ceremony: Have a well dressed, handsome bagpiper in his dress kilt pipe you and the haggis into the dining room. Another well-dressed kilt wearer wielding a sword to stop foreigners who have been attracted to the aroma should accompany the Haggis. Serve hot with chappit (mashed potatoes) and neeps (rutabagas) and serve Atholl Brose (recipe in This and That) as your dinner beverage.

Bobby Burns' Poem About Haggis: This is difficult to read because of the thick brogue but here are the passages of which Scotland is so proud:

"Fair fa' your honest, sonsie face,
Great chieftain o' the puddin' race!
Aboon them a' ye tak your place,
Painch, tripe, or thairm;Weel are ye worthy of a grace
As lang's my airm…
Ye Powr's, wha mak mankind your care,
And dish them out their bill o' fare,
That jaups in luggies;
But, if ye wish her gratfu' prayer,
Gie her a Haggis!"

"Some people wanted champagne and caviar when they should have had beer and hot dogs." Dwight D. Eisenhower (1890-1969)

Hamburger A La Mode

Vincent Price (1911-1993) once wrote out his favorite hamburger recipe in longhand for a friend. This surprisingly simple recipe is actually quite an elegant hamburger.

"Hamburger done the way you like it. Top with sour cream and caviar and dress with chopped onion or sliced green onion."

*"This is the church where we sing Amen
At the end of every song.
The coffee pot is always on
Cause the meetings are three hours long.
The blessed tie that binds our hearts
Is cream of mushroom soup.
We do not walk through the door alone.
We wait and go as a group."*
Garrison Keiller

Hamburger Pie

Greta Manville, who co-authored *The Purgatory Trail,* and is currently on a fellowship to complete a bibliography of criticism about John Steinbeck, offered this unusual recipe.

- 1 pound hamburger
- 1/3 cup chopped onion
- 1 can mushroom soup
- 5-6 sliced mushrooms
- 1 soup can water
- Salt to taste
- 6-8 unbaked biscuits (not frozen type)

Brown hamburger. Add onion and simmer until translucent. Stir in soup, mushrooms, water and salt. Thoroughly mix, then pour mixture into wide, shallow casserole dish. Top with 6-8 unbaked biscuits. Bake at 425 degrees for 12-15 minutes until biscuits turn golden brown. Serves 4.

"The public buys its opinions as it buys its meat, or takes in its milk, on the principle that it is cheaper to do this than to keep a cow. So it is, but the milk is more likely to be watered." Samuel Butler (1835-1902)

Hot Dogs

Vincent Price (1911-1993), actor, art connoisseur, chef and cookbook author, humorously titled this recipe "Buried Alive Hot Dogs." He had starred in many horror films such as *Abbott and Costello Meet Frankenstein, House of Wax, The Fly, The Tingler, The Bat, Pit and the Pendulum, The Raven, Thriller, Edward Scissorhands, The Abominable Dr. Phibes,* etc.

Just before the latter film was released, a caption under a horrifying picture of Vincent as Dr. Phibes said, "Love means never having to say you're ugly." It was a take-off on a line from the movie *Love Story,* "Love is never having to say you're sorry." This recipe was on the Internet.

- 1 cup pineapple juice
- ½ cup chili sauce
- 1 tablespoon dried bell peppers
- ½ teaspoon English mustard
- 2 tablespoons wine vinegar
- ½ teaspoon garlic salt
- 2 tablespoons soy sauce

- 1 tablespoon molasses
- 2 tablespoons minced sautéed onion
- 6 large frankfurters
- 6 heated rolls or buns

Combine the first 9 ingredients in a skillet and simmer 20 minutes. Preheat the oven to 350 degrees. Cut diagonal slashes across 6 large frankfurters. Put them in a baking pan and cover with sauce (but save enough sauce for a few spoonfuls over each hot dog in final presentation.)

Bake frankfurters for 40 minutes, basting with the sauce several times to keep them from drying out. Place frankfurters in heated rolls with a few spoonfuls of sauce spread over each.

The frankfurters may be eaten without rolls using a knife and fork if preferred, in which case they are truly "buried alive" in the sauce.

"When the stomach is full, it is easy to talk of fasting." St. Jerome (342-420)

Kedgeree

Vincent Price (1911-1993) was often seen on cooking shows after he wrote his book *A Treasury of Great Recipes.* He was a wonderful guest for the Paul Lynde Cooking Show, (yes, the comedian Paul Lynde,) Dinah Shore Show, Julia Child Show, Helen Corbitt Show, and many others.

This dish came from the English with a touch of India, where the English reigned for many years. This recipe is available on the Internet.

- 1 pound can of salmon OR
- 1 ½ pounds poached salmon

- 2 tablespoons butter
- 1 medium onion, chopped
- 1 teaspoon salt
- 1 cup rice
- 1 can chicken consommé plus water to equal 2 cups
- 1 hard boiled egg, diced
- ½ cup béchamel sauce
- Salt to taste
- 1 tablespoon butter

Flake the salmon to make 2 cups. Set aside.

Preheat oven to 350 degrees. In a saucepan melt 2 tablespoons butter and sauté the onion for 5 minutes. Add salt, rice, and consommé to make a rice pilaf. Bring to a boil. Cover tightly and cook over low heat without stirring for 30 minutes. Remove the cover, stir, and let steam for 5 minutes more.

Mix 1 cup of the rice pilaf with 1 cup of the flaked salmon. Add the egg, béchamel sauce and salt. Make a ring of this mixture in a glass baking dish, 8" round and 2" deep. Fill the center with the remainder of the flaked salmon and cover with the remaining rice. Dot with the remaining tablespoon of butter.

Set the dish in a pan containing 1" hot water. Cover the baking dish with greased brown paper or foil and bake for 20 minutes. Serve with your favorite curry sauce.

"Tell us how the dinner is prepared with lamb meat and meat portions. With the lamb omentum you can wrap yourself and burn thus to relieve us from your questions." Plato (428-347 B.C.)

Lamb Kidneys Bourguignon

Rex Stout (1886-1975) described this recipe in his Nero Wolfe mystery, *Counterfeit for Murder.* He included the recipe in his *Nero Wolfe's Cookbook.*

While it does not contain lamb omentum, (in the quotation from Plato above) if washed in water and cooked adequately, it will be cleansed from questions of urine aroma. This recipe is available on the Internet.

- 18 lamb kidneys
- ½ cup flour
- Salt and freshly ground pepper
- 6 tablespoons butter
- 2 shallots, minced
- ½ pound mushrooms, minced
- 2 cups dry red wine
- ½ bay leaf
- 1 tablespoon watercress, minced
- 1 tablespoon celery, minced
- ¼ teaspoon thyme

Soak the kidneys in cold water for 10 minutes. Remove the membranes and connective tissue and cut the kidneys across in half. Season the flour with the salt and pepper and dredge the kidneys. Sauté them in 4 tablespoons of the butter and set aside.

Add the shallots and mushrooms to the butter. Sprinkle with 2 tablespoons of the dredging flour and cook over low heat for 5 minutes, stirring occasionally.

Add the wine, bay leaf, watercress, celery, thyme, ½ teaspoon salt, and a few grindings of black pepper. Stir well and add the kidneys; cover the skillet and simmer gently for 25 minutes.

When ready to serve, remove the bay leaf, add the remaining 2 tablespoons of butter and correct the seasoning. Serve over rice. Serves 6.

"The only real stumbling block is fear of failure. In cooking you've got to have a what-the-hell attitude." Julia Child

Leg of Lamb

Alice B. Toklas, lover and promoter of Gertrude Stein in Paris during the 1920s and 1930s, wrote *The Alice B. Toklas Cookbook, Aromas and Flavors of Past and Present, What Is Remembered,* and various other books.

Originally a pianist who considered a career as a concert pianist, she met Stein's brother and accepted an invitation to meet Gertrude which changed her life. The two of them collected the works of artists such as Picasso, Gris and Matisse, which were made available to museums upon their death.

Alice obtained this recipe from the cook of a French surgeon who lived in the French provinces. At first she did not believe that a syringe was necessary to inject liquids into the lamb until she found the method described in a collection of outstanding French recipes.

- Leg of lamb
- Marinade of red wine and virgin olive oil

- Salt, pepper, bay leaf, thyme
- A knob of ginger root grated
- A pinch of cayenne
- A nutmeg cut into small pieces
- A handful of crushed juniper berries
- ¾ teaspoon powdered sugar
- 1 large syringe
- ½ cup cognac or more
- ½ cup fresh orange juice or more
- Option: 2 tablespoons of a hare's blood

"Eight days in advance you will cover the leg of mutton with the marinade called Baume Samaritain composed of wine (burgundy Beaune or Chambertin) and virgin olive oil. Into this balm to which you have added the usual condiments of salt, pepper, bay leaf, thyme, beside an atom of ginger root, put a pinch of cayenne, a nutmeg cut into small pieces, a handful of crushed juniper berries and lastly a dessertspoon of powered sugar which serves to fix the different aromas. Twice a day you will turn the leg of lamb.

"Now we come to the point of preparation. After you have placed the leg in the marinade, you will arm yourself with a surgical syringe of a size to hold one cup which you will fill with half a cup of cognac and half a cup of fresh orange juice. Inject the contents of the syringe into the fleshy part of the lamb leg in three different spots. Refill the syringe with the same contents and inject twice more.

"Each day you will fill the syringes with the marinade and inject the contents into the lamb's leg. At the end of the week the leg of lamb is ready to be roasted. Roast and serve with the usual lamb or venison sauce to which has been added just before serving 2 tablespoons of the blood of a hare."

"Kissing don't last; cookery do!" George Meredith (1828-1909)

Liver Casserole

Cat Stevens, British singer and composer, loved a bit 'er liver. He created a children's book that also became an animated cartoon called *Teaser and the Firecat* This recipe appeared in the February 3, 1973 issue of British Magazine *POPSWOP,* and it is available on the Internet.

- 1 pound lamb's liver
- Salt and pepper
- 2 onions sliced
- 2 tablespoons cornflour (cornmeal)
- 2 tablespoons corn oil
- 2 ounces mushrooms, sliced
- 1 packet Knorr mushroom soup
- 2 ounces peas
- 1 pint of water

Trim the liver and coat with cornflour to which salt and pepper have been added. Heat corn oil in a frying pan, add the liver and brown well on both sides. Remove to a casserole. Gently fry the onions and mushrooms in the remaining corn oil. Place over the liver.

Add the contents of the mushroom soup packet and the water to the pan. Bring to a boil and stir. Pour over the liver. Bake at 375 degrees for 45 minutes. Fifteen minutes before the end of the cooking time, add the peas. Serve it with some luv'ly mashed potatoes—it's just too much!

"Luxurious lobster nights, farewell,
For sober, studious days!
Alexander Pope (1688-1744)

Lobster

William Makepeace Thackeray (1811-1863) was born in India but resided in the British Isles for most of his life. He was a novelist and satirist best known for writing *Vanity Fair, Henry Esmond* and the *Book of Snobs.* He described verbatim how to clean and shell lobsters much larger than are commonly available today.

- 1 lobster per person
- ½ pound butter
- 1 tablespoon catsup
- 1 cup vinegar (white wine)
- Dash cayenne pepper to taste
- 8 or so ounces of sherry

"You take a lobster, about three feet long if possible, remove the shell, cut or break the flesh of the fish in pieces not too small. Someone else meanwhile makes a mixture of mustard, vinegar, catsup and lots of cayenne pepper. You produce a machine called 'despatcher' which has a spirit lamp underneath it that is usually illuminated with whiskey."

(He appears to be talking about a chafing dish with a flame.)

"The lobster, the sauce and near half a pound of butter are placed in the despatcher, which is immediately closed. When boiling, the mixture is stirred up, the lobster being sure to heave about the pan in a convulsive manner, while it emits a remarkable rich and agreeable odour through the apartment. A glass and a half of sherry is now thrown into the pan, and the contents served out hot, and eaten by the company. Porter (i.e. Stout) is commonly drunk, and whisly-punch afterwards, and the dish is fit for an emperor."

Note: This makes a rather sour taste and some might prefer to substitute ½ cup of white wine for ½ cup of vinegar.

"Jack Sprat could eat no fat, his wife could eat no lean'
And so, betwixt them both, they licked the platter clean." Mother Goose

Meatloaf

Garrison Keillor, often called the modern Mark Twain, wrote various books about Lake Wobegon, and has regularly appeared on the radio and television. This recipe is from "A Prairie Home Companion" web site.

"I never see meatloaf on the menus of the restaurants I go to, and maybe I'm going to the wrong restaurants. The ones I patronize tend to offer you grilled mahi-mahi on a bed of basmati rice lightly drizzled with cilantro crème fraiche. Which can be good in its own way, but as deep fall comes on and the first snowfall lurks in the wings, I somehow long for a good meatloaf dinner. And that's why we serve it for the Prairie Home Companion Opening Night Street Dance. It can be cold on that first Saturday in October. Snow can fall. People who intend to dance in the street need a supper more substantial than mahi-mahi. My mother, Grace Keillor, made excellent meat loaf, which she adapted from the Betty Crocker cookbook."

- 1 ½ pounds of lean ground beef
- 3 slices of bread, diced

- ½ cup milk
- 2 eggs beaten
- ¼ cup minced onion
- ¼ teaspoon pepper
- ¼ teaspoon celery salt
- ¼ teaspoon garlic salt
- ¼ teaspoon dried mustard
- ¼ teaspoon sage

"Bake in a loaf pan for 1 ½ hours at 350 degrees. You can put ketchup on the top if you wish. The Betty Crocker recipe calls for one pound of ground beef, ¼ pound lean ground pork and ¼ pound ground veal. And Worcestershire sauce, which usually my mother skips. Maybe nowadays she uses it, though. In recent years her children have accompanied her on trips to luxurious places, the Ritz Hotel in London, the Sherry Netherland in New York, and perhaps Worcestershire is now on her list. For the street dance, however, we'll do with the basics. Dance bands, hot coffee, ground beef. The sun goes down on October 6 and a crowd of Minnesotans dances to Zydeco and rockabilly in the street. It's different, all right."

"There was no getting around the stubborn fact that taking sweetmeats was only 'hooking,' while taking bacon and hams and such valuables was plain simple stealing, and there was a commandment against that in the Bible."
Mark Twain (1835-1910)

Meatloaf

Ann Landers (1918-2002) wrote a syndicated column in newspapers for over 40 years, offering advice to the lovelorn, playing advocate and counsel, and opposer of racism and bias. Her parents were Russian Jewish immigrants who arrived in this country to give birth to twin girls. Her sister's penname is Abigail Van Buren. The sisters had a double wedding when they married for the first time.

Ann (Eppie) was looking for a job as she moved around the country with her husband and contacted the Sun Times in Chicago to ask if Ann Landers needed any help with her column, which had been running for 12 years. She was unaware that the Sun Times was looking for a replacement for Ann Landers and she got the job. Shortly her sister began writing a similar column for another newspaper and the two tried but could not avoid acrimonious competition with each other.

This simple recipe appeared in one of her columns and many asked her to repeat it several times. The recipe is also available on the Internet.

- 2 eggs
- 1 ½ cups bread crumbs
- ¾ cup ketchup
- 1 teaspoon Accent (optional)
- ½ cup warm water
- 1 envelope onion soup mix
- 8 ounce can tomato sauce
- 2 pounds ground round
- 2 slices bacon

Combine the first six ingredients. Add ground beef and mix well. Put into a pan. Cover with 2 strips bacon, if desired. Pour tomato sauce over the top. Bake at 350 degrees for 1 hour.

"Little Miss Muffet sat on a tuffet,
Eating her curds and whey
Along came a spider and sat down beside her,
And frightened Miss Muffet away."
Mother Goose

Mrs. Bianco's Ravioli

Lois Gentry is a short story writer from Peoria, Illinois. Lois said that her mother's heritage of French and German and her father's hill country background made her words come out all backwards. She is now living in Arizona completing her first novel and has written many short stories. She wrote about Mrs. Bianco, a family friend whom she knew in 1938.

"If I shut my eyes I can still see her apron wrapped around her short body and beautiful ebony eyes that crinkled with laughter. When I was six, she taught me the fine art of stirring pots and tasting. My job was to stand on a kitchen chair and stir and stir and stir everything she added to the pot. Then I would be offered a taste so I could pass judgment. Those tastes were delicious and are fond memories."

- 1 #303 can of spinach
- 1 pound small curd cottage cheese
- 3 eggs
- 1 cup parmesan cheese
- Cracker crumbs, ground fine
- Garlic salt
- 3 cups all purpose flour
- 3 eggs, slightly beaten

Put the spinach and cottage cheese in a strainer and allow all liquid to drain for one hour. Place the mixture in a large bowl and add the eggs, Parmesan, crumbs, garlic salt and mix well. Set aside.

To make the dough, put the flour in a large bowl. Make a well and put in the eggs. Stir until incorporated and noodle consistency. Take ½ of the mixture and turn it out on a lightly floured board. Roll thin. Cut 3x3 inch pieces and put some filling into the center of each. Do not over fill. Moisten the edges of each square and fold corner to corner, pressing closed with fingers or fork. Set these aside and continue with the other half.

Bring to a rapid boil a 4-quart pot of salted water. Drop about 8 to 10 ravioli at a time into the water. Cool al dente. Drain well and put in a serving bowl.

When all the ravioli are cooked, pour over the top some hot tomato sauce seasoned with garlic salt to taste. Sprinkle liberally with Parmesan cheese. Enjoy.

"To make an omelet, you have to be willing to break a few eggs." Robert Penn Warren (1905-1989)

Omelet

Alexander Dumas (1802-1870) the author of *The Three Musketeers, Count of Monte Cristo, Man in the Iron Mask,* also wrote *The Dictionary of Cuisine* in 1873, published posthumously. Dumas' son wrote the famous novel, *Camille.*

Dumas was actually North African, and enjoyed early success with his writings. He moved into a chateau, had many mistresses, built up debts and spent the remainder of his life writing to pay off his debts. He also established a Parisian newspaper called "The Musketeer" after his famous novel. Because he enjoyed food so much, he was quite corpulent in his later years and would fall asleep during meals, awaken, eat some more, and sleep again.

An example of the wit and excellent writing in Dumas' cuisine book is captured in this phrase about a recipe for truffles. "The truffles themselves have been interrogated, and have answered simply: eat us and praise the Lord."

This recipe is a version of Dumas' omelet as prepared by Darrell Ray and is available on the Internet.

- 2 eggs
- ½ clove chopped shallots
- ¼ lemon
- ¼ cup grated Jalapeno Jack pepper cheese
- ¼ cup diced red pepper
- ½ cup sliced Crimini, Shitake and Oyster mushrooms
- 1 tablespoon sour cream
- 2 pats butter
- 1 teaspoon lemon juice
- Salt and fresh ground pepper.

Beat eggs with 1 tablespoon of water, not milk. Water will make them cook up fluffier. In a non-stick pan, melt one pat of butter over low heat. Then crank up the heat to medium high and pour in the eggs. Immediately reduce heat to low, and season.

In another pan, melt the other pat of butter over low heat and add the shallots. Sweat them but don't let them brown, then add red peppers and mushrooms. Season with salt and pepper.

When the omelet has a little wetness on top, carefully flip the eggs and reduce the heat to very low. Grate your pepper cheese directly over the pan onto the omelet. When the peppers, mushrooms and shallots have wilted, add the lemon juice and stir. Drain any extra fat from the pan. Ladle the filling onto the melted cheese in your omelet and carefully fold and cook for a few more moments. Place on a plate with a dollop of sour cream on top. Dumas recommended garnish with a serving of absinthe but the nearest we can come is a tiny glass of ouzo or raki served ice cold.

"A tale without love is like beef without mustard: insipid." Anatole France (1844-1924)

Over the Sink Sandwich

Lawrence Sanders (1920-1998) wrote about retired N.Y.P.D. Chief of Detectives, Edward X. Delaney. Sanders turned to fiction after some 20 years of writing for scientific journals such as *Mechanics Illustrated, Science and Mechanics*, etc. The source for this interesting concoction is Sanders book, *The Third Deadly Sin.*

"Former Chief of Detectives Edward X. Delaney had two methods of eating sandwiches.

"Those he categorized as 'dry' sandwiches, such as roast beef on white or what he termed an interracial sandwich, ham on bagel, were eaten while seated at the kitchen table. The top was spread with the financial section of the previous day's *New York Times.*

"Wet sandwiches, such as potato salad and pastrami on rye, with hot English mustard, or brisling sardines with tomato and onion slices slathered with mayonnaise, were eaten while standing bent over the sink. Finished, Delaney ran the hot water and flushed the drippings away...."

"Actually, he loved sandwiches. One of the recurring fantasies of his increasingly onerous retirement was the dream that he might one day compile a slim volume, *Chief Delaney's Sandwich Book*. Who had a better right? Who but he had discovered the glory of cold pork and thinly sliced white radish on pumpernickel?"

"The pig, if I am not mistaken
Supplies us sausage, ham and bacon.
Let others say his heart is big,
I call it stupid of the pig."
Ogden Nash (1902-1971)

Pork Casserole

Danny Kaye (1913-1987), entertainer, writer, UNESCO volunteer, and gourmet chef called this recipe "Lion's Head." It appeared in Craig Claiborne's *The New New York Times Cookbook*.

Danny wrote *Danny Kaye's around the World Story Book, The Enchanted World of Danny Kaye,* and the chapter about Hans Christian Andersen in *Scope and Treatment: The New Book of Knowledge.*

- 8 dried black mushrooms
- 1 ¼ pounds ground pork
- 20 water chestnuts, diced
- 1 teaspoon minced ginger
- 3 scallions, chopped
- 1 teaspoon garlic, minced
- 1 orange rind grated

- ¼ teaspoon sesame oil
- 1 tablespoon dry sherry
- 1 tablespoon soy sauce
- 1 teaspoon salt
- 1 tablespoon cornstarch
- Oil (peanut or corn)
- Steamed spinach or broccoli (optional)

Place mushrooms in mixing bowl and add hot water to cover. Let stand 20 minutes or until soft. Put pork in another bowl. Drain mushrooms and squeeze dry. Chop them and add to pork. Add chestnuts, ginger, scallions, garlic, rind, sesame oil, sherry, garlic, soy, salt and cornstarch. Mix and shape in 8-12 balls.

Heat oil and fry balls until crisp and golden. Drain. Place in steamer and steam 20-25 minutes. Serve on spinach or broccoli. Serves 8.

"Few would dispute the thesis that food, properly cooked and served, and of course adapted to the hour, is attractive four times in the day. But to a large proportion among us, even sausages and marmalade at nine... would prove not only not attractive but positively repellent if offered us on a small steamer on a rough day." Julian Huxley (1887-1975)

Potatoes and Sausage

Ernest Hemingway (1899-1961) often visited the Brasserie Lipp in Paris and ordered one dish over and over. It was called "Potatoes in Oil and Mustard Sauce," and he referred to it in his "Moveable Feast." This recipe is on the Internet in Daniel Rogov's Column.

He wrote, "The beer was very cold and wonderful to drink. The potatoes in oil were firm and marinated and the olive oil was delicious. I ground black pepper over the potatoes and moistened the bread in the oil. After the first heavy draught of beer I drank and ate very slowly, and when the potatoes were gone I ordered another serving and a Cervalas, a sausage-like heavy, wide frankfurter split in two and covered with mustard sauce. I mopped up all of the oil and all the sauce with bread and drank the beer slowly until it began to lose its coldness, and then I finished it and ordered another."

- 3 tablespoons olive oil
- 1 tablespoon vinegar
- 1 tablespoon sugar
- 2 cloves garlic, chopped fine
- 6 green onions, diced
- 1 teaspoon powdered mustard
- Salt and pepper to taste
- 4 medium potatoes
- 1 tablespoon parsley, chopped, for garnish
- 4-6 radishes
- French bread for serving
- 2 Cervalas or Knockwurst sausage

In a small bowl, combine the oil, vinegar, sugar, garlic, onions, mustard, salt and pepper. Whip, and then cover and let stand at room temperature 1-2 hours.

In a large saucepan with lightly salted boiled water, cook the potatoes until done but still firm. Remove from the water and peel. Allow the potatoes to cool until lukewarm and cut into 1 inch squares.

Pour the dressing over the potatoes, toss lightly, let stand, covered, at room temperature for about one hour. Cook the sausage, and split in half lengthwise.

Sprinkle parsley over the potatoes and serve with French bread, radishes and warm sausage. Serves 2.

"If I had to give young writers advice, I'd say don't listen to writers talking about writing." Lillian Hellman

Pot Roast

Lillian Hellman was the daughter of a shoe salesman and grew up by going back and forth between her parents in New York City and her aunts in Louisiana. She attended NYU and Columbia but early left to review books for the New York Herald Tribune. She published some short stories and went to Hollywood to read movie scripts for MGM. Her seven-year marriage failed and she began a 30-year on and off affair with Dashiell Hammett.

She was a smoker, a drinker, a lover, and fighter. When called to testify before the House Un-American Activities in 1952 she said, "I will not cut my conscience to fit this year's fashions."

She wrote *The Children's Hour, The Little Foxes, Days To Come, Watch on the Rhine, Another Part of the Forest, Toys in the Attic, Pentimento* (made into the movie *Julia*), etc.

Dashiell Hammett wrote the Sam Spade and the Nick and Nora Charles "Thin Man" mysteries and based Nora on Lillian.

Hellman also co-authored *Eating Together* in 1984. This recipe comes from her cookbook.

- 4-5 pound pot roast
- 10 ounce can cream of mushroom soup
- 1 envelope onion soup mix
- 10 ounces red wine
- 10 ounces water
- 1 onion, chopped
- 2 cloves garlic, minced
- 1 bay leaf
- 1 teaspoon thyme
- 1 teaspoon basil

Put the pot roast in an ovenproof casserole. Combine all the other ingredients and pour them over the meat. Cover tightly with foil. Bake at 350 degrees for 3 ½ hours.

"A crust eaten in peace is better than a banquet partaken in anxiety." Aesop (6th century B.C.)

Quiche

Barry Goldwater (1909-1998), senator of Arizona and presidential candidate, ran on a platform of nuclear aggression. He also ran a bed and breakfast later after he lost the presidential election. He prepared many wonderful dishes.

Besides writing the introduction and/or preface for over ten books, he wrote some other books. Among these are *Delightful Journey, The Conscience of a Conservative* and *With No Apologies.* This recipe, thanks to Bessie Lipinski, appeared in *Bed and Breakfast in Arizona* and is on the Internet.

- 1 9-inch pie shell, partially baked
- 1 ½ cups grated Jack cheese
- 1 cup grated mild Cheddar cheese
- 1 can (4 ounces) diced green chilies
- 1 cup half and half
- 3 eggs, slightly beaten
- ½ teaspoon cumin

Preheat oven to 450 degrees. Bake pie shell for five minutes. Reduce heat to 325 degrees. In a small mixing bowl, combine Jack cheese with ½ cup Cheddar cheese and spread over pie shell. Sprinkle chilies over the cheese. Combine half and half, eggs, salt and cumin; pour carefully into pie shell.

Top with remaining Cheddar cheese. Bake for 40-50 minutes. Serves 6. Gently shake quiche to test for doneness.

"And if that ain't true, grits ain't groceries, eggs ain't poultry, and Mona Lisa was a man." Henry "Peter Rabbit" McGarrh, 1978

Rabbit Diane

Dr. Diane Holloway, Dallas psychologist, writer, and editor of this book, was once served "Saddle of Hare Diane" in a Dallas restaurant called *La Vielle Varsovie* or *Old Warsaw*. She was so elated that she was served a famous dish with her name that she persuaded the restaurant to give her the recipe.

- 2 rabbits
- Salt
- Ground black pepper
- Slices of salt pork
- Olive oil
- Chestnut puree*
- Sauce Diane**
- Garnish with watercress or parsley

Rub the rabbit with salt and pepper. Cover with slices of salt pork and pour enough oil into a roasting pan to cover the bottom generously. Heat in a preheated oven (450 degrees) until oil is smoking, then put in the meat. Roast 18-20 minutes. Transfer meat to a heated platter. If desired, chop the salt pork and garnish the top.

Serve with Chestnut Puree and/or Sauce Diane. Makes 6 servings.

*Chestnut Puree:
- 1 pound shelled cooked chestnuts
- 2 tablespoons butter
- Salt and pepper
- Heavy cream

Put chestnuts through a food chopper using the finest blade. Then force through a sieve. Add butter, salt and pepper. Thin with heavy cream to consistency desired. Makes 1 ½ cups.

**Sauce Diane
- 2 tablespoons butter
- 2 tablespoons minced shallots
- Splash of Brandy

- Splash of dry vermouth or cognac
- 1 tablespoon Dijon mustard
- 8 ounces cream
- Bay leaves or thyme

Put butter and shallots in saucepan to cook until tender. Carefully flame pan with brandy then vermouth or cognac. Follow with the mustard, cream, and herb. Let simmer until it starts to thicken. Add salt and pepper. Serve on top of the rabbit.

"There is no flavor comparable, I will contend, to that of the crisp, tawny, well-watched, not over-roasted, crackling, as it is well called, the very teeth are invited to their share of the pleasure at this banquet in overcoming the boy, brittle resistance-with the adhesive oleaginous, O call it not fat, but an indefinable sweetness growing up to it." Charles Lamb (1775-1834), from "A Dissertation Upon Roast Pig."

Roast Pork Castilian Style

Vincent Price (1911-1993) had a full rich life earning two degrees in art, three wives, over 100 films, and several books to his credit. This recipe is from his book *A Treasury of Great Recipes*. He picked up this recipe in his travels to Madrid. This recipe is available on the Internet.

- 12-14 pounds of fresh ham
- 4 tablespoons butter or shortening
- 3 crumbled bay leaves
- 3 garlic cloves, minced

- ½ teaspoon dry thyme
- 2 teaspoons salt
- 2 tablespoons chopped parsley
- 3 tablespoons minced onion
- Juice of one lemon
- 2/3 cups white wine (used 1/3 at a time)
- 2 tablespoons sweet paprika

Preheat the oven to 350 degrees. Score the skin and fat of a fresh ham. Place in a shallow roasting pan and rub the skin with butter or shortening. Mix the bay leaves, garlic, thyme, parsley and onions and sprinkle over the meat. Sprinkle the meat with lemon juice, 1/3 cup white wine, paprika and salt.

Roast for 1 ½ hours. Remove fat that has accumulated in the pan. Add to the pan 1/3 cup white wine, 1 cup water.

Roast another 3 ½-4 ½ hours longer, baste every half hour with liquid in the pan.

"Beulah, peel me a grape." Mae West (1893-1980)

Roast Quail Veronique

Rex Stout (1886-1975) was discovered to be a child prodigy in arithmetic at an early age. After high school, he went to the University of Kansas for a while but left to join the Navy. He had the unusual post of warrant officer aboard Theodore Roosevelt's yacht for two years. Following that, he was a sightseeing guide and itinerant bookkeeper.

He entered the world of finance and designed a school banking system, which came to be used in over 400 U.S. cities. He took his finance earnings and went to Paris in 1927 to write. After establishing the Nero Wolfe mystery novels, he waged war against Nazism upon his return to the U.S. He was an emcee on the radio's "Speaking of Liberty" program.

After WWII, he attempted to lead the public in opposing thermonuclear devices. He wrote a total of 73 Nero Wolfe mysteries before he died.

He included this recipe in his *Nero Wolfe's Cookbook.* This might best be prepared during quail season as it was in his mystery novel. This recipe is available on the Internet.

- 6 quail, dressed
- Salt and fresh ground pepper
- 1 ½ cups wild rice, cooked
- ½ cup butter, melted
- 2/3 cup dry white wine
- ½ cup veal bouillon
- ½ cup peeled green seedless grapes
- 12 small slices bread (homemade will do)
- ½ pound boiled ham

Preheat the oven to 450 degrees. Wash and wipe the quail dry. Rub the insides with salt and pepper. Stuff each bird with the wild rice mixed with a little of the melted butter. Truss with butcher's cord. Put the quail in a shallow roasting pan, brush with butter, and roast for 5 minutes at 450 degrees. Lower the heat to 325 and roast for 20 minutes more, basting with additional butter. When done, remove from the pan and keep warm on a platter.

Deglaze the pan with the wine and veal bouillon and bring to a boil. Lower the heat and add the grapes. Simmer 5 minutes and correct the seasonings.

Fry the bread in a little butter and cut into triangles. Arrange the toast on a serving platter and cover with julienned slices of ham. Place the quail on top and spoon some of the sauce over them. Serve the rest of the sauce in a sauceboat. Serves 6.

"1948 was the year the first McDonald's restaurant opened, thus beginning the era of 'fast food.' Instead of forcing customers to waste valuable time waiting while their orders were prepared from fresh ingredients, the restaurant decided ahead of time what the customers wanted (they wanted meat fried in grease, with a side order of potatoes fried in grease) and prepared the food well in advance." Dave Barry

Sausage with Wine

Inspector Jules Maigret was the creation of Georges Simenon (1903-1989.) Maigret enjoyed cuisine and dined well in Paris while working on cases in the Simenon series. French readers embraced these mysteries and created recipes using Simenon descriptions of Maigret's meals. One such creation is this recipe, which is available on the Internet.

- ½ kilo well spiced sausages, sliced
- 6 tablespoons dry white wine
- 2 pimientos cut in strips
- 2 tablespoons parsley, chopped
- 3-4 cloves garlic, minced.

In a large heavy skillet, sauté the sausages until lightly browned. Pour off most of the fat. Pour in the wine and scrape the pan well over a flame. Add the remaining ingredients and transfer to a baking dish in a medium oven (350 degrees) for 15 minutes. Serve hot. Serves 2-4.

"A meal without wine is like a day without sunshine." Anthelme Brillat-Savarin (1755-1826)

Scallops

Rex Stout's (1886-1975) most famous protagonist, Nero Wolfe, liked seafood. This recipe is in Stout's *Nero Wolfe's Cookbook* and is available on the internet.

- 1 cup dry white wine
- 1 cup water
- 1 bay leaf
- 6 black peppercorns
- 1 pound bay scallops
- 5 tablespoons butter
- 1 tablespoon shallots, minced
- 3 tablespoons flour
- 1 teaspoon salt
- 1 sprig parsley
- 1 pinch nutmeg
- 2 tablespoons parsley, chopped
- Butter
- 1 tablespoon lemon juice
- ½ cup fresh bread crumbs
- ¼ cup Gruyere cheese, grated

Heat oven to 350 degrees. In a large saucepan, bring wine and water to boil. Add the bay leaf, peppercorns and thoroughly cleaned scallops. Return to boil, reduce heat and simmer 3-4 minutes. Drain scallops, reserving broth.

In small heavy-bottomed pan, melt 3 tablespoons of the butter and cook minced shallots until translucent, but not browned. Add flour and stir constantly until it starts to turn golden. Gradually stir in 1 cup reserved hot broth. Continue to cook, stirring constantly, until the sauce thickens. Add ½ teaspoon of the salt, sprig of parsley and nutmeg, and cook a few more minutes. Strain the sauce into a bowl.

Add the scallops, chopped parsley, lemon juice and remaining ½ teaspoon salt. Stir well. Butter 4 baking shells and divide scallop mixture evenly among them. Combine bread crumbs and grated cheese. Sprinkle over filled shells. Dot with remaining 2 tablespoons of butter.

Bake 20-25 minutes or until tops are golden brown. Note: This may be prepared in a casserole rather than four baking shells. Serves 4.

"There is always a best way of doing everything, even if it be to boil an egg. Manners are the happy ways of doing things." Ralph Waldo Emerson (1803-1882)

Scrambled Eggs

British singer, composer and musician, Cat Stevens is best known in America for his hit tune *Morning Has Broken*. He contributed this recipe to a Messena, New York fundraising event for boy scouts in 1981. They published the cookbook under the title of *Scouts and Celebrity Stew*. This recipe is available on the Internet.

- 3 eggs
- A knob of butter (1 tablespoon)
- A pinch of salt
- 2 tablespoons of milk or cream

Melt the butter in a saucepan. Break 2 eggs into the saucepan. Take a third egg and separate the yolk from the white. Put only the white into the saucepan with the other two eggs. Add cream or milk. Increase stirring as eggs harden.

Finally when the eggs are scrambled, add egg yolk just before serving but do not cook any more. Add a touch of parsley for a garnish. Serves one.

"Some hate broccoli, some hate bacon.
I hate having my picture taken."
Ogden Nash (1902-1971)

Shrimp and Grits

John Grisham, author of such novels as *The Pelican Brief* and *The Firm,* wrote an article for the Little Rock Junior League Cookbook, *Apron Strings,* and titled it "In Defense of Grits." He obviously loved bacon in his grits.

"One of our guests made a profane comment about grits. Though I tried not to show it, I was deeply wounded by what was said. I vowed revenge. I called my friend, John Currence, the chef of my favorite restaurant in the world, the City Grocery in Oxford, Mississippi, and he faxed me his recipe for Shrimp and Grits. John has prepared this dish for us a thousand times, and we've even begun cooking it ourselves.

"When our guests inquired about the main course for dinner, I simply said we were having grits. They went for a long walk. Renee added extra bacon to the recipe, and I loaded up on the cayenne pepper and the Tabasco. Our guests said nothing when we served them in the candlelight.

Since they are our friends, they began by picking at the dish, their noses still pointed to the North. They ate like refugees. I've never seen two Yankees so gorge themselves on grits. But, I've never known one recipe do so much for such a humble food."

Here is John Currence's Shrimp and Grits recipe.
- 2 cups chopped smoked bacon
- 3 tablespoons olive oil
- 1 ½ pounds shrimp
- Salt and pepper
- 1 tablespoon minced garlic
- 3 cups sliced white mushrooms
- 2 tablespoons lemon juice
- 3 tablespoons white wine
- 2 cups sliced scallions
- Cheese grits

Cook the bacon in a skillet until it begins to brown. Remove the bacon with a slotted spoon to drain and reserve 2 tablespoons drippings. Heat a large skillet until very hot. Add the oil and reserved bacon drippings and heat until the oil begins to smoke. Add the shrimp and sprinkle immediately with salt and pepper. Sauté until the shrimp turn pink and the skillet has returned to the original temperature.

Add the garlic and bacon. Cook for several minutes, stirring to prevent over-browning. Add the mushrooms and sauté briefly. Add the lemon juice and wine. Cook for 30 seconds, stirring constantly. Add the scallions and sauté for 20 seconds; do not brown. Serve over cheese grits. Enjoy, burp, and reminisce. Serves 3 or 4.

Cheese Grits:
- 1 cup quick-cooking grits
- ¼ cup unsalted butter
- ¾ cup shredded extra-sharp white Cheddar cheese
- ½ cup grated Parmesan cheese
- 1 teaspoon cayenne
- 1 ½ tablespoons paprika
- 1 teaspoon Tabasco
- Salt and pepper to taste

Cook the grits using the package directions. Whisk in the butter, cheeses, cayenne, paprika and Tabasco sauce. Season with salt and pepper. Keep warm until serving time. Serves 3 or 4.

"Are you going to Scarborough Fair;
Parsley, sage, rosemary and thyme.
Remember me to one who lives there.
She once was a true love of mine."
Olde English verse.

Swordfish

Aaron E. Hotchner (A. E.) likes to tell people that he was born in St. Louis and grew up in the Westgate Hotel. He attended Washington University where he earned a law degree. He practiced law for two years and then joined the Air Force where he was asked to write, among other things, the script for a movie that would portray the Anti-submarine Command's role in combating U-boats.

He wrote *Papa Hemingway, King of the Hill, Louisiana Purchase, The Man Who Lived at the Ritz, Looking For Miracles, Welcome to the Club, Exactly Like You, The White House, The Hole in the Wall Gang Cookbook* and over 300 pieces and short stories for *Esquire, Saturday Evening Post,* and *Readers Digest.*

He and actor Paul Newman have accidentally created a food empire through products and cookbooks that benefit children with cancer.

Hotchner and Ernest Hemingway used to eat at a little restaurant at Torremolinas in Spain, run by a Basque fisherman. Hotch wrote, "We were so smitten by this swordfish that I asked the old man to show me how to cook it. I once tried to cook it on a grill in Ketchum, Idaho (where Hemingway killed himself) but the swordfish was frozen and had no taste… Make sure the pine bough has not been sprayed with pesticides. Rinse and dry it well before using."

- 2 pounds swordfish steak, 2" thick
- 1 cup Newman's Salad/Vinaigrette Dressing
- ¼ cup fresh lime juice
- 3 tablespoons fresh thyme or rosemary
- Lemon juice
- Butter
- 1 small freshly cut pine bough
- Fresh parsley

Marinate the swordfish in the salad dressing, lime juice and thyme or rosemary for several hours in the refrigerator. Prepare a charcoal grill and place the fish on the grill. Saturate with lemon juice, chunks of butter, and more thyme. Cook for 10 minutes on each side, turning only once. Baste with more lemon juice and marinade, and dot with butter after turning.

Remove the fish, place the pine bough on the fire, put the fish on top, and let it be seared by the flame. Remove after the pine flame dies down and serve immediately. Garnish with fresh parsley. Serves 4-6.

*"Where the apple reddens, never pry
Lest we lost our Eden's, Eve and I."*
Robert Browning (1812-1889)

Tournedos Rossini

Giacchino Rossini (1792-1868) is most famous for his operas such as *William Tell* and *The Barber of Seville*. But he was well known to chefs and writers as a gourmand. Biographer Stendhal said that the aria "Di tanti palpiti" from his opera *Tancredi* was known throughout Europe as the "rice aria" because he composed it while waiting for a risotto in a Venice restaurant.

Rossini also composed some little piano pieces called "Radishes," "Anchovy," "Pickles," "Butter," "Dry Figs," "Almonds," "Raisins," and "Hazelnuts." Ottorino Respighi included some of them in his ballet *La Boutique Fantasque*.

The chef at a Parisian restaurant who knew that turkey stuffed with truffles was Rossini's favorite dish created this recipe and it is available on the Internet.

- 1-2 tablespoons butter
- 4 slices duck or goose liver
- 4 slices toasted white bread without crusts
- 4 beef tournedos (or thin filet mignons)
- 1-2 tablespoons olive oil
- 3 garlic cloves, sliced finely

- ½ cup brown demi-glace sauce*
- 2 sliced truffles or mushrooms of choice
- 1-2 tablespoon Madeira or rich red wine
- Apple

In a hot frying pan, mix the butter and oil. Season the beef pieces with salt and pepper and fry rapidly to seal. In another pan, rapidly fry the duck or goose liver and place on absorbent paper.

Braise the truffles or mushrooms in a little butter with 1-2 spoonfuls of Madeira wine. Add the brown sauce and let simmer for 3 minutes. Keep hot.

*To make brown sauce, in the pan deglaze the meat with a few drops of port, a few of brandy, a few of Madeira wine and a few ounces of veal stock. Allow to reduce. If you choose not to make a brown sauce, use ½ cup of Madeira wine instead.

Prepare the plates by placing the tournedos with the slice of liver and the truffles or mushrooms on top, on a slide of bread. Cover everything in sauce. Serve immediately. Serves 4.

If desired, top dish with an apple with an arrow through it, the way it was served to Rossini when he completed *William Tell* in 1829.

"Oh, the roast beef of England
And old England's roast beef."
Henry Fielding (1707-1754)

Wellington

Vincent Price (1911-1993) enjoyed fine food, fine art, fine friends, and entertained with great relish. The 6'4 actor enjoyed a close relationship with smallish actor Edward G. Robinson, who also had a very fine art collection. Price and Robinson competed enjoyably on the topic of art on the television program, *The $64,000 Challenge.*

He had an interesting variation on the usually expensive Beef Wellington making it more like a meatloaf. He said, "Juicy beef in a light pastry shell is one dish sure to make guests flake out. And it doesn't have to cost a fortune." This recipe is available on the Internet.

- 2 packages pie crust mix
- 2 onions, chopped
- 1 8-ounce can drained dropped mushrooms
- 1 cup bread crumbs
- 2 eggs
- 2 tablespoons Angostura aromatic bitters
- 2 teaspoons salt
- 2 pounds ground beef

Prepare the packages of piecrust according to the directions. Roll out into 10 x 14 inch oblong shape. Sauté the onion and mushrooms. Add to the bread crumbs, mix with eggs, bitters and salt. Mix with ground beef and shape into an oblong loaf. Place the meat loaf on the crust. Moisten the edges of the piecrust and fold completely around the meat, leaving ½ inch hole in the top of the crust at the seam for grease to flow out.

Place seam side down on greased cookie sheet. Bake for 1 ½ hours at 350 degrees. Lift carefully once done. Serve attractively on a bed of parsley with cherry tomatoes.

"Life, within doors, has few pleasanter prospects than a neatly arranged and well-provisioned breakfast table." Nathaniel Hawthorne (1804-1864)

Yorkshire Buck

Rex Stout's (1886-1975) Nero Wolfe novel, *The Doorbell Rang,* included this English-style cheese and egg dish. The recipe is in Stout's *Nero Wolfe's Cookbook.* This makes the perfect exceptional breakfast and little else is needed but fruit to flesh out a full meal. But since it's English, tea should be served with it. This recipe is available on the Internet.

- 1 tablespoon butter
- 1 pound Cheshire cheese, grated
- 1 cup ale (not beer)
- 7 large eggs
- ¼ teaspoon salt
- 1 teaspoon dry mustard
- 2 dashes Tabasco
- 6 slices Canadian bacon
- 3 English muffins
- 2 tablespoons Dijon mustard

Melt the butter in the top of a double boiler. Add the cheese and as it begins to melt, add the ale slowly, stirring constantly. Beat 1 of the eggs and add it, along with the salt, dry mustard and Tabasco. Continue to stir until the cheese is melted and the mixture is smooth. Lower the heat and keep hot.

Poach the remaining 6 eggs and keep them warm while you fry the bacon on a griddle.

Split and toast the English muffins and spread them with a thin coating of Dijon mustard. Put the muffins on a serving plate, pour on the cheese, and top with a slice of bacon, a poached egg, and some more cheese. Serve as hot as possible.

Run the muffins under a hot broiler to glaze the tops, if you like. Serves 6.

Chapter 6

BLACK TURKEY

The History of This Recipe

This chapter is devoted to one recipe. It is the longest recipe and the most complex of any in this book. But the humorous style in which it is written is priceless. And after all, this cookbook is devoted to writers.

Morton Thompson was primarily a reporter and correspondent but he wrote two books, *Not As A Stranger*, which was made into a movie, and *Joe, the Wounded Tennis Player*, a collection of funny pieces published in 1945. In the latter, he included this recipe.

He had earlier given the recipe to Robert Benchley, actor, humorist and writer. Benchley had eaten the turkey, liked it, loved the funny recipe, and intended to publish it but lost it. Thompson didn't want to go through the travail of writing it up for Benchley again, but did for his own 1945 book.

This recipe is a subject of great interest and even Martha Stewart has published it, along with countless others. But no version of the writing or the recipe compares with Thompson's original version described here.

Those who have prepared this turkey rave about its wonderful taste despite its blackened charred look at the outset. There is one caveat, however. Other testers have found that a turkey over 20 pounds is just too heavy to maneuver through the various steps.

Morton Thompson's Black Turkey

This turkey is work...it requires more attention than an average six-month old baby. There are no shortcuts, as you will see.

Get a huge turkey. I don't mean just a big, big bird, but one that looks as though it gave the farmer a hard time when he did it in. It ought to weigh between 16 and 30 pounds. Have the poultry man, or butcher, cut its head off at the end of the neck, peel back the skin, and remove the neck close to the body, leaving the tube. You will want this for stuffing. Also, he should leave all the fat on the bird.

When you are ready to cook your bird, rub it inside and out with salt and pepper. Give it a friendly pat and set it aside. Chop the heart, gizzard, and liver and put them, with the neck, into a stew pan with a clove of garlic, a large bay leave, ½ teaspoon coriander, and some salt. I don't know how much salt; whatever you think. Cover this with about 5 cups of water and put on the stove to simmer. This will be the basting fluid a little later.

About this time I generally have my first drink of the day, usually a Ramos Fizz. (See this recipe under beverages.) Save your egg yolks, plus 1 teaspoon of the lemon; you'll need them later. Have a good sip!

Get a huge bowl. Throw into it one diced apple, one diced orange, a large can of crushed pineapple, the grated rind of a lemon, and three tablespoons of chopped preserved ginger. Add 2 cans of drained Chinese water chestnuts.

Mix this altogether and have another sip of your drink. Get a second, somewhat smaller, bowl. Into this, measuring by teaspoons, put:

- 2 teaspoons hot dry mustard
- 2 teaspoons caraway seed
- 2 teaspoons celery seed
- 2 teaspoons poppy seed
- 1 teaspoon black pepper

- 2 ½ teaspoons oregano
- ½ teaspoon mace
- ½ teaspoon turmeric
- ½ teaspoon marjoram
- ½ teaspoon savory
- ¾ teaspoon sage
- ¾ teaspoon thyme
- ¼ teaspoon basil
- ½ teaspoon chili powder
- 1 tablespoon poultry seasoning
- 4 tablespoons parsley
- 1 tablespoon salt
- 4 crushed cloves
- 1 well-crushed bay leaf
- 4 large chopped onions
- 6 good dashes Tabasco
- 5 crushed garlic cloves
- 6 large chopped celery

Wipe your brow, refocus your eyes, get yet another drink, and a third bowl. Put in three packages of unseasoned bread crumbs (32 ounces), ¾ pound ground veal, ½ pound ground fresh pork, ¼ pound of butter, and all the fat you have been able to pull out of the bird.

About now it seems advisable to switch drinks. Martinis or stingers are recommended. Get a fourth bowl, an enormous one. Take a sip for a few minutes, wash your hands, and mix the contents of all the other bowls. Mix it well. Stuff the bird and skewer it. Put the leftover stuffing into the neck tube.

Turn your oven to 500 degrees and get out a fifth small bowl. Make a paste consisting of those four egg yolks and lemon juice left from the

Ramos Fizz. Add 1 teaspoon hot dry mustard, a crushed clove of garlic, 1 tablespoon onion juice, and enough flour (1-2 tablespoons) to make a stiff paste. When the oven is red hot, put the bird in, breast down on the rack. Sip on your drink until the bird has begun to brown all over, then take it out and paint the bird all over with paste. Put it back in and turn the oven down to 350 degrees. Let the paste set, then pull the bird out and paint again. Keep doing this until the paste is used up.

Add 2-3 cups cider or white wine to the stuff that's been simmering on the stove. This is your basting fluid. The turkey must be basted every 15 minutes. Don't argue. Set your timer and keep it up.

When confronted with the choice "do I baste from the juice under the bird or do I baste with the juice from the pot on the stove?" make certain that the juice under the bird neither dries out and burns, nor becomes so thin that gravy is weak. When you run out of baste, use cheap red wine. This critter makes incredible gravy. The bird should cook about 12 minutes per pound, basting every 15 minutes (could be 6 ½-7 hours.) Enlist the aid of your friends and family.

As the bird cooks, it will first get a light brown, then a dark brown, then darker and darker. After about 2 hours you will think I'm crazy. The bird will be turning black. Newcomers to black turkey will think you are demented and drunk on your butt, which, if you've followed instructions, you are. In fact, by the time it is finished, it will look as though we have ruined it.

Take a fork and poke at the black cindery crust. Beneath, the bird will be a gorgeous mahogany, reminding one of those golden-browns found in precious Rembrandts. Stick the fork too deep, and the juice will gush to the ceiling. When you take it out, ready to carve it, you will find that you do not need a knife. A loud sound will cause the bird to fall apart like the walls of that famed biblical city. The moist flesh will drive you crazy, and the stuffing—well, there is nothing like it on this earth. You will make the gravy just like it is always done, adding the giblets and what is left of the basting fluid.

Sometime during the meal, use a moment to give thanks to Morton Thompson. There is seldom, if ever, leftover turkey when this recipe is used. If there is, you'll find that the fowl retains its moisture for a few days. That's all there is to it. It's work, hard work, but it's worth it.

Chapter 7

VEGETABLES AND SIDE DISHES

Sweet Corn

Sweet corn was our family's weakness. We were prepared to resist atheistic Communism, immoral Hollywood, hard liquor, gambling and dancing, smoking, fornication, but if Satan had come around with sweet corn, we at least would have listened to what he had to sell. We might not have bought it but we would've had him in and given him a cup of coffee…. People have searched the world over for something better and didn't find it because it's not there. There's nothing better, not even sex. People have wanted sex to be as good as sweet corn and have worked hard to improve it, and afterward they lay together in the dark, and said 'That was so wonderful. But it wasn't as good as fresh sweet corn'. Garrison Keillor *Leaving Home*

"The cheery noise of bubbling pancake batter was as plainly heard as the singing teakettle every morning of the year in our house. I often lifted the cover of the batter crock to look at the bubbles, which reminded me of the eyes of animals." V. P. Hedrick

Blinis Demidof

Isak Dinesen's (1885-1962) story of *Babette's Feast* (she also wrote *Out of Africa)* was made into a movie with such outstanding dishes that it won the 1997 Cinema and Food Retrospective Festival in Italy for the "best on screen recipes."

This is a version of the most complex of the award-winning recipes. It was called Blinis Demidof. Blinis are pancakes and Demidoff is the addition of sliced carrots and/or other vegetables cooked in butter and added to a dish.

This recipe is a yeasted pancake made with gingered carrots and beets. Members of the Theater Oobleck in Chicago who put on the play recently created this version so they could serve it to the audience during the course of the play.

- 1 teaspoon active dry yeast
- 2 ¾ cups all purpose flour
- 3 ¼ cups warm milk
- 4 eggs, separated
- ¼ teaspoon salt
- ¾ inch chunk fresh ginger, grated
- 4 medium beets, tops removed
- 6-7 teaspoons horseradish
- 1 tablespoon cider vinegar
- 2 tablespoons orange juice

- ½ teaspoon sugar
- 1 cup grated carrots
- Clarified butter
- Salt and pepper
- Sour cream

In a large bowl, stir together the yeast, ½ cup of the flour and 2 cups of the milk. Cover and set aside in a warm place for 30 minutes. Let the remaining milk cool to lukewarm.

Beat the egg yolks and stir into the yeast mixture with the remaining milk and flour and ¼ teaspoon salt.

Beat the egg white to stiff peaks and fold into the batter. Cover and let rest in a warm place to rise for 1 hour.

Cook the beets until tender in a large pot of boiling salted water. Peel, then grate or chop the beets and combine them with the horseradish, vinegar, orange juice and sugar. Set aside in the refrigerator.

Meanwhile, in a large skillet over low heat, sauté the ginger and carrots in clarified butter until just warmed through. Season with salt and pepper. Let cool.

Fold ¾ cup of the cooled carrot mixture into the blini batter.

Heat a nonstick skillet, brush lightly with clarified butter and cook a few blini at a time. Make them 3-4 inches in diameter. Cook for 1 to 1 ½ minutes, then flip and cook the other side about 1 minute, until puffed and golden.

Serve warm, topped with sour cream and the carrot-beet mixture. Makes about 40 blini, or 10-15 servings.

"The human waistline will succumb
To such and such a diet.
The ladies gnaw on carrots raw,
Their husbands will not try it."
Ogden Nash (1902-1971)

Carrots

Nero Wolfe, Rex Stout's (1886-1975) detective, was never one to watch his waistline. This recipe for Nero Wolfe's Carottes Flamandes, was described in the novel *The Father Hunt*. It is in the *Nero Wolfe Cookbook* by Stout and is available on the Internet.

- 1 pound carrots
- ¼ cup cold water
- 8 tablespoons butter
- ¼ teaspoon salt
- 3 tablespoons sugar
- 1 tablespoon orange rind, grated
- 3 egg yolks
- ½ cup heavy cream
- 1 tablespoon parsley, chopped
- 2 tablespoons sweet butter, melted

Wash and scrape the carrots, cutting them into 1-inch sections and trimming the ends. Blanch them in boiling water to cover for 5 minutes, drain and place in a well-buttered casserole. Add the cold water and butter, and season with salt and sugar. Cover the casserole and bring the liquid to a boil. Reduce the heat and continue to cook the carrots for 20 minutes or longer until they are tender. Shake the casserole every 5 minutes or so to prevent the carrots from sticking to the pan.

Five minutes before the carrots are done, add the orange rind and stir. When the carrots are cooked, remove them from the heat. Mix the egg yolks with the cream, parsley and melted butter. Add the mixture to the casserole stirring gently, and put back over a low flame. When the sauce begins to thicken (do not let it boil), remove from the heat and serve. Serves 6.

"Any man who hates dogs and loves whiskey can't be all bad." W. C. Fields (1880-1946)

Cauliflower and Whiskey

This traditional Scottish recipe was well known to Sir Walter Scott (1722-1832) who wrote *Ivanhoe, Kenilworth, The Bride of Lammermoor,* and many other works. It was a combination of cauliflower, cheese, oatmeal and whiskey.

He referred to such a dish in his novels and this recipe is available on the Internet.

- 1 cauliflower
- 6 ounces chopped mushrooms
- ½ green pepper finely chopped
- 10 ounces (300ml) cream
- 4 ounces grated sharp cheddar cheese
- 3 ounces Scotch whiskey
- 1 ounce fine oatmeal

- Pinch of nutmeg
- Salt and pepper
- 2 ounces (1/2 cup) chopped mixed nuts

Remove cauliflower stalks and cook the florets in hot water for five minutes. Drain and put in ovenproof dish with the mushrooms and green peppers mixed in.

Heat the cream gently in a small pan, add the cheese, stirring frequently. When the cheese has melted, remove from heat and mix in the whiskey and oatmeal. Add salt and pepper to taste and nutmeg pinch.

Pour over the cauliflower and sprinkle the chopped nuts on top. Bake in preheated oven at 350 degrees for 45 minutes. Serve immediately. Serves 4 to 6.

"The proof of the pudding is in the eating." Miguel de Cervantes (1547-1616)

Corn Pudding

Rex Stout (1886-1975), author of the Nero Wolfe novel, *Too Many Cooks*, referred to this recipe, which he called "Green-Corn Pudding." The recipe is in his *Nero Wolfe's Cookbook*, and this recipe is available on the Internet.

- 6 ears very young corn
- 1 tablespoon sugar
- 1 tablespoon cornstarch
- 1 teaspoon salt
- 2 tablespoons pimiento, chopped

- 3 large eggs
- 4 tablespoons butter, melted
- 1 cup milk

Preheat oven to 350 degrees. Combine all ingredients in the order given except for the eggs.

Separate the eggs, beating the yolks and adding them to the mixture. Beat the egg whites until stiff and fold them in last. Put the mixture into a greased 1 ½ quart casserole and bake for 35 minutes.

Optional: Add 1 cup of cooked chicken and omit the sugar. Serves 6.

"Why doesn't someone write a cookbook for the suburban woman with one car that is used by her husband? Some real clever woman could call it "Cookbook for the Suburban Woman With One Car That Is Used by Her Husband." Erma Bombeck

Fake-It Casserole

Erma Bombeck (1927-1996) wrote many books and columns about humor. In *Forever, Erma*, she said if she ever wrote a cookbook, she would include this recipe.

"You substitute a cup of noodles for a cup of asparagus. Then for the sour cream, you either add a tablespoon of vinegar to the milk you have on hand to curdle it or forget about it entirely and add a can of cream of mushroom soup. If you don't have cream of mushroom soup, put in a cup of grated cheese. However, if you have the mushroom soup, add bread-crumbs and some minced onion. If you have the cheese but not the soup, sprinkle a little Parmesan on top and slip it into the oven.

"Bake it at 350 degrees for 20 minutes if you've the noodles and the sour cream, or at 325 degrees for 30 minutes if you've the asparagus and the grated cheese. If this recipe makes you tense, then for goodness' sake forget it and have pork chops and applesauce."

"Vegetables are interesting but lack a sense of purpose when unaccompanied by a good cut of meat." Fran Lebowitz

Fried Green Tomatoes

Fannie Flagg, actress, screenwriter, director and author, wrote a story made into a movie about four women who describe their lives. One says, "I would give anything to eat a plate of fried green tomatoes like the ones at the Whistle Stop." The Whistle Stop Café has published their recipe and Fannie has included it in her new cookbook, *Fannie Flagg's Original Whistle Stop Café Cookbook.*

Here is one Internet version of the recipe. Source for the hornworm recipe: David George Gordon's *Eat-A-Bug Cookbook.*

- 6-8 large green tomatoes
- 1/3 cup flour
- ½ cup vegetable or olive oil
- Salt and pepper

Wash, core and cut the tomatoes into thick slices. Dredge them in the flour. Heat the oil but not so much that it darkens. Cook the tomatoes five minutes on one side and five minutes on the other side. Remove to paper towels to absorb fat. Season with salt and pepper.

Now some people like to fry up the Fried Green Tomato Hornworms. Use the same method and fry the hornworms and tomatoes about four minutes, taking care not to rupture the insects. Top each fried tomato with two hornworms and a basil leaf but don't serve them to me.

"Life is like an onion: You peel it off one layer at a time, and sometimes you weep." Carl Sandburg (1878-1967)

Lenten Chili

Vincent Price (1911-1993), movie actor, artist, author, and cookbook author, suggested this dish for Lent, which is available on the Internet.

- 1 package corn muffin mix
- 2 tablespoons butter
- Cup chopped onion
- 1 can tomatoes
- 1 tablespoon chili powder
- Salt and pepper to taste
- 2 cans dark kidney beans, drained
- 1 cup each Cheddar, Jack, Monterrey shredded cheese

Preheat oven to 350 degrees. Prepare muffin mix according to directions. Bake in sprayed or buttered 8 or 9 inch square pan. Cool on a wire rack 15 minutes. Meanwhile melt 2 tablespoons butter in a saucepan. Sauté onions until golden. Stir in tomatoes and seasonings.

Simmer 15 minutes. Stir in beans, simmer 10 more minutes, remove from heat. Stir in cheeses. To serve, place cornbread on plates and smother with tomato, bean, cheese mixture. Serves 4.

"I come from a family where gravy was considered a beverage." Erma Bombeck (1927-1996)

Macaroni and Cheese

Ronald Reagan, former actor, Governor of California, American President and author, wrote *Where's the Rest of Me, Abortion and the Conscience of the Nation, Ronald Reagan: An American Life,* and *Reagan In His Own Hand.* Raised by an alcoholic salesman father and religious mother, Reagan was not interested in fine dining. His wife, Nancy, said that this was one of his favorite recipes.

- ½ pound macaroni
- 1 teaspoon butter
- 1 egg, beaten
- 1 teaspoon dry mustard
- 1 teaspoon salt
- 1 tablespoon hot water
- 1 cup milk
- 3 cups shredded cheese

Boil macaroni in water until tender; drain thoroughly. Stir in butter and egg. Mix mustard and salt with hot water; add to milk. Add cheese to macaroni, leaving enough to sprinkle on top.

Pour macaroni and cheese into a buttered 1-quart casserole; add milk mixture; sprinkle with reserved cheese.

Bake at 350 degrees for about 45 minutes or until custard is set and top is crusty." Serves 6 to 8.

"Madam, there's no such thing as a tough child. If you parboil them first for seven hours, they always come out tender." W. C. Fields (1880-1946)

Potatoes in Oil and Mustard

In the 1930s, Ernest Hemingway (1899-1961) described life in Paris as "an experience beyond beauty." He would sit at the Brasserie Lipp, start with a beer, and then order potatoes in oil and mustard sauce. This recipe and information is on the internet.

"The beer was very cold and wonderful to drink," he wrote in *A Moveable Feast*. "The potatoes in oil were firm and marinated and the olive oil was delicious. I ground black pepper over the potatoes and moistened the bread in the oil. After the first heavy draught of beer I drank and ate very slowly, and when the potatoes were gone I ordered another serving and a cervesa, a sausage-like heavy, wide frankfurter split in two and covered with the mustard sauce. I mopped up the oil and all of the sauce with bread and drank the beer slowly until it began to lose its cold, then I finished it and ordered another."

"With coarse rice to eat, with water to drink, and my bended arm for a pillow, I have still joy in the midst of these things." Confucius (551-479 B. C.)

Rice

Ronald Reagan, former actor, spokesman for General Electric, Governor of California, and American President, starred in several movies before he started his political career. He was in *Knute Rockne: All American, King's Row, The Hasty Heart, This Is the Army, Santa Fe Trail, Dark Victory, Bedtime for Bonzo, The Killers,* and many others.

He was a success in every area of his life except with his children. He admitted that he lacked the ability to be close enough to them, and they confirmed that.

He contributed this recipe to the U.S. Bicentennial commemorative cookbook when he was the governor of California. He called it "Rancho California Rice."

- 1 cup onion, chopped
- 4 tablespoons butter
- 4 cups rice, cooked
- 2 cups sour cream
- 1 cup cottage cheese
- 1 bay leaf, crumbled
- Salt and pepper to taste
- 16 oz. whole green chilies (canned)
- 2 cups grated cheddar cheese

Sauté onions in butter until limp. Add rice, sour cream, cottage cheese, bay leaf and salt and pepper. Mix well. In greased casserole dish, put a layer of rice mixture, a layer of chilies (seeded and cut into strips) ending with a layer of rice. Bake for 25 minutes at 375 degrees. Top with remaining cheese and bake 10 more minutes.

"Everything you see, I owe to spaghetti." Sophia Loren

Spaghetti

Sophia Loren, Italian movie actress, has written a cookbook called *Sophia Loren Recipes and Memories*. About this recipe called "Spaghetti

Con Pomodoro Crudo" or spaghetti with uncooked tomato sauce, Sophia said, "This is cool and refreshing, excellent for summer. Serve with chilled white wine."

The surprise in this recipe is the lack of cooking of anything but the pasta. This recipe is available on the Internet.

- 1 ½ pounds spaghetti
- 2 pounds tomatoes, not quite ripe, chopped
- ½ pound mozzarella cheese, thinly sliced
- 2 medium red or Vidalia onions, thinly sliced
- ¼ cup pitted green olives, roughly chopped
- 2 tablespoons drained capers
- ¼ cup minced Italian parsley
- 10-12 fresh oregano leaves chopped
- 1-2 cloves garlic, crushed
- Freshly ground pepper
- 1/3 cup extra virgin olive oil
- Freshly grated Parmesan cheese (optional)

Cook pasta until al dente. While cooking, place tomatoes, mozzarella, onions, olives, capers, parsley, oregano, garlic, salt and pepper in a serving bowl. Pour the oil over and toss gently.

When the pasta is ready, pour into a colander and rinse under cold water quickly. Drain and add the warm spaghetti to the bowl. Toss, serve, and pass the cheese at the table. Serves 6.

"It's broccoli, dear." "I say it's spinach, and I say the hell with it." E. B. White (1899-1985)

Spinach

Ladybird Johnson kept a diary while her husband, Lyndon, was President. She published *A White House Diary* in 1970 through Henry Holt & Company. She was a loyal and supportive wife to her sometimes philandering and ever braggardly husband. She had many recipes of note and this is one, which is available on the Internet.

- 3 pounds spinach, washed, drained, cooked, OR
- Substitute 2 packages frozen spinach if preferred
- 6 tablespoons Parmesan cheese
- 6 tablespoons minced onion
- 6 tablespoons light cream or half and half
- 4 tablespoons melted butter
- Salt and pepper
- ½ cup cracker crumbs
- 1 tablespoon melted butter

Cook the spinach, drain it and chop it coarsely. Add the Parmesan, onion, cream, butter, and seasoning. Place in a shallow butter 1 ½-2 quart baking dish and sprinkle with crumbs that have been mixed with 1 tablespoon melted butter.

Bake in a preheated oven at 375 for 10-15 minutes or until golden and lightly crusted. If Saltine crackers are used, they have a lot of salt so be careful when salting the dish. Serves 4 to 6 people as a side dish.

Chapter 8

BREAD AND ROLLS

Bread

"We were so afraid the poor people might drink, now we fixed it so they can't eat. Is Japan and China's troubles more to us than our bread line? We got more wheat, more corn, more food, more cotton, more money in the banks, more everything in the world than any nation that ever lived had, yet we are starving to death, we are the first nation in the history of the world to go to the poorhouse in an automobile. We been so busy in the last few years getting radios and bathtubs and facial creams, that we forgot to see if we had any bacon and beans." Will Rogers during the Depression.

"You tell me whar a man gits his corn pone, en I'll tell you what his 'pinions is." Mark Twain (1835-1910)

Ash Cake

Mark Twain (1835-1910) had a very simple remedy to get rid of unwanted guests or tramps. He made his famous Ash Cake or cornpone (cornbread.) How long would you hang around if served this concoction?

"Take a lot of water and add to it a lot of coarse Indian meal and about a quart of a lot of salt. Mix well together, knead into the form of a pone, and let the pone stand awhile, not on its edge, but the other way. Rake away a place among the embers, lay it there and cover it an inch deep in hot ashes. When it is done, remove it; blow off all the ashes but one layer; butter that one and eat. No household should ever be without this talisman. It has been noticed that tramps never return for another ash-cake."

"I cannot forebear mentioning a very offensive custom of putting milk, and a variety of medicines in the waters at the pump (spa), which then become mere vehicles, their specific properties being destroyed by the mixture." Dr. W. Oliver

Bath Buns

Dr. William Oliver (1695-1764) was born and educated in England where he became a physician. He went to Bath in 1728, famous for its mineral water, and the Bath Hospital was a place where physicians all over the world sent patients when they didn't know what else to do with them. He founded the Bath General Hospital where patients were treated.

Oliver wrote medical articles on such conditions as gout, but he wrote other works as well. In 1753, he published a "pastoral" called *Myra* and he was the anonymous author of *A faint sketch of the life, manner and character of the late Mr. Nash.* Oliver Goldsmith praised the latter work as "written with much good sense and still more good nature."

Dr. Oliver invented a rich, sweet bun that his patients adored. Unfortunately, they ate too many and undid all the good of his treatment. Being a good businessman, he then cunningly invented a plain biscuit for his patients, which was not as fattening as the buns. These are known today as Bath Oliver biscuits. This recipe makes 12 delicious biscuits, which are sometimes eaten with cheese.

Batter:
- 5 ounces flour (150 g.)
- 1 teaspoon sugar
- 2 teaspoons dried yeast
- ½ cup hot milk
- ½ cup less 4 tablespoons hot water

Dough:
- 11 ounces flour (300 g.)
- 2 ounces, diced butter
- 2 eggs, beaten
- 1/3 cup sugar
- ¾ cup raisins
- ¼ cup lemon and orange peel

Egg Glaze:
- 1 egg
- 1 teaspoon sugar

- 1 tablespoon water
- 3 tablespoons crushed sugar cubes

Place the batter ingredients in a bowl. Beat until smooth, then leave in a warm place until frothy for about 20 minutes.

For the dough, place the flour in a bowl and rub in the butter until the mixture resembles breadcrumbs. Add that to the eggs, sugar, raisins and peel and then blend with the batter. Beat well for about 10 minutes.

Cover and leave to rise for about 1 ½ hours or until the dough has doubled in size and will spring back when lightly pressed.

Preheat oven to 425 degrees and lightly butter 2 baking sheets. Beat the dough well for a few minutes with a wooden spoon. Place tablespoonfuls of the dough on the baking sheets. Cover and leave in a warm place for 30 minutes until double in size.

Place the egg, sugar and water in a bowl and beat until well mixed.

Uncover the buns and brush with the egg glaze and sprinkle with crushed sugar cubes. Bake for 15 to 20 minutes. Leave to cool on a wire rack.

"A book of verses underneath the bough,
A jug of wine, a loaf of bread,
And thou beside me singing in the wilderness,
Oh, wilderness were paradise enow."
Edward Fitzgerald, (1809-1883) Rubiyat of Omar Khayyam

Bread

Before bread machines, Mary and Vincent Price's (1911-1993) cookbook, *A Treasury of Great Recipes,* offered the best recipe for bread imaginable. Too bad that he and Mary divorced when he fell in love with his third wife, or many other culinary texts might have resulted.

Vincent called this recipe "House Bread" and said it has a taste and texture of real French bread. Cooks seem to agree as they rave about it. For a special treat, serve it warm with garlic butter and chopped parsley and chives. This recipe is available on the Internet.

- 5 cups flour
- 1 package of active dry yeast
- 2 cups warm water
- ½ teaspoon powdered ginger
- 2 teaspoons salt
- 1 tablespoon sugar
- 2-4 tablespoons melted butter
- ¼ cup yellow cornmeal
- Baking sheet buttered, dusted with cornmeal
- Small bowl of ice water

Place 2 cups of flour in a bowl and add the ginger, salt and sugar. Mix with the flat beater on low until well mixed. Then add yeast and mix again. Add the warm water and slowly increase mixer speed to medium high and mix until smooth or about 2 minutes.

Add the rest of the flour ½ cup at a time until the dough becomes a shaggy mass too dense for the beater and mix with a large wooden spoon of some sort.

Keep adding flour and mixing until the dough forms a ball and cleans the sides of the bowl. Knead 8 to 10 minutes until the dough is smooth and elastic, adding sprinkles of flour to keep the dough from sticking. Place in a warm bowl coated with soft butter, turn once to butter the top, cover with plastic wrap and let rise until double in size.

Punch down, knead a few times to work out the air bubbles and form into one large or two small loaves, French bread style. Place them on the cookie sheets coated with butter and dusted with cornmeal. With a sharp knife, slash the loaves across the top with a few diagonal cuts. Brush the loaves with ice water using a pastry brush. Place the loaves in a warm, draft-free place and allow to rise until doubled.

Preheat oven to 450 degrees. For a great crust, place a pan of boiling water on the bottom of the oven and brush each loaf with melted butter. Bake for 7 minutes, then reduce heat to 350 degrees and bake for 35-45 minutes longer.

"Some girls can bake a pie,
Made of prunes and quinces;
Some may an oyster fry
Others are good at blintzes.
Some lovely girls have done
Wonders with turkey stuffin's,
But I have found the one
Who can really make corn muffins."
Ira Gershwin (1896-1983) in "Of Thee I Sing," a Pulitzer Prize winning musical which opened in 1931, about a girl who prided herself in making corn muffins without corn.

Cornbread

Marjorie Kinnan Rawlings (1876-1953) wrote *The Yearling* and *Cross Creek Country*. The latter book included a recipe for Custard-Filled Cornbread. A creamy barely set custard forms and people will wonder exactly what it is. Rawlings' version was a little sweeter than this one. This recipe is available on the Internet.

- 2 eggs
- 3 tablespoons butter, melted
- 3 tablespoons sugar (or more)
- ½ teaspoon salt
- 2 cups milk
- 1 ½ tablespoons white vinegar
- 1 cup all-purpose flour
- ¾ cup yellow cornmeal
- 1 teaspoon baking powder
- ½ teaspoon baking soda
- 1 cup heavy cream

Preheat the oven to 350 degrees. Butter an 8-inch square baking dish that is 2 inches deep. Put the buttered dish in the oven and let it get hot while you make the batter. Put the eggs in a mixing bowl and add the melted butter. Beat until well blended.

Add sugar, salt, milk, and vinegar and beat well. Sift or stir together in a bowl the flour, cornmeal, baking powder, baking soda, and add to the egg mixture. Mix until the batter is smooth. Pour into the heated dish and then pour the cream into the center of the batter. Don't stir! Bake for 1 hour or until lightly browned. Serve warm.

"Breakfast: a mighty porterhouse steak an inch and a half thick, hot and sputtering from the griddle; dusted with fragrant pepper; enriched with little melting bits of butter; the precious juices of the meat trickling out and joining the gravy, archipelagoed with mushrooms; and a great cup of American homemade coffee…some smoking-hot biscuits, a plate of hot buckwheat cakes, with transparent syrup." Mark Twain (1835-1910)

Corn Pancakes with Tomato Cheese Sauce

Rex Stout (1886-1975) included this in his *Nero Wolfe's Cookbook*. He had two separate recipes, one for corn cakes and the other for corn cakes with tomato and cheese sauce. While usually served at breakfast, this could make an accompaniment to an evening meal.

This version combines both and allows the cook to decide whether to prepare the sauce. This recipe is available on the Internet.

- 2 cups corn meal (see notes below)
- 1 cup all-purpose flour
- 1 teaspoon baking powder
- ¼ teaspoon powdered sage
- 1 ½ teaspoons salt
- 4 tablespoons butter
- 2 large eggs
- ¼ cup minced celery
- 3 cups milk

Combine the corn meal, flour, baking powder, sage and salt in a bowl. In a small skillet melt the butter and sauté the celery until soft.

Beat the eggs and add to the corn meal with the celery and butter. Mix well. Gradually add the milk, stirring constantly until the batter is the thickness of heavy cream.

Heat the griddle, grease it, and pour out the batter by spoonfuls to make cakes about two inches in diameter. Turn once so they are nicely browned on both sides. Add more milk to the batter if it begins to thicken. Serve as a side dish with plenty of butter.

Notes: If you are making the sauce, use white corn meal. If not, use yellow corn meal. Additionally, you may choose to eliminate the sage and celery if you are using the sauce.

Tomato and Cheese Sauce:
- 2 tablespoons butter
- 2 tablespoons all-purpose flour
- 1 ½ cups heavy cream
- ¼ pound Fontina cheese
- 2 egg yolks
- ½ cup tomato puree
- ½ teaspoon salt
- 2 grindings black pepper
- 2 dashes Tabasco (optional)

Melt the butter in a saucepan and add the flour. Cook over a low heat for 3 minutes, stirring, and gradually add the cream, stirring constantly.

Cube the cheese and add to the sauce, a few cubes at a time, until it is all melted. Remove from heat.

Beat the egg yolks with a little of the sauce and then add to the saucepan. Stir well over low heat until the sauce has thickened.

Add the tomato puree and stir until heated through. A tiny pinch of sugar may be desired to tame the acidity of the tomato puree. Season with salt and pepper. Add the Tabasco if you like a hotter sauce. Makes about 18 pancakes with sauce topping.

"Take wheat and barley, beans and lentil, millet and spelt; put them in a storage jar and use them to make bread for yourself." Ezekiel 4:9

Croissants

Tennessee Williams (1911-1983) wrote *A Streetcar Named 'Desire'* while staying in the Maison de Ville Hotel in New Orleans (in a room which had been slave quarters before the Civil War.)

Tennessee Williams (Thomas Lanier Williams) was born to a shoe salesman and a minister's daughter in Columbus, Mississippi. He eventually attended the University of Missouri for a short time but became a shoe salesman. His writing finally paid off and he wrote a succession of famous works made into movies: *Glass Menagerie, Summer and Smoke, A Rose Tattoo, Cat On a Hot Tin Roof, Night of the Iguana,* and many others.

His regular breakfast fare at Maison de Ville was café au lait and croissants. His café au lait was made using half chicory coffee and half hot milk with sugar. This was the recipe used by the Maison de Ville for croissants during the time that Williams was there.

- 2 envelopes active dry yeast
- ¼ cup lukewarm water
- 1 ½ tablespoons sugar
- 4 cups sifted all-purpose flour
- 1 ½ cups lukewarm milk
- 1 teaspoon salt
- ¾ pound butter
- 1 egg yolk beaten with 1 tablespoon milk

Soften yeast in lukewarm water with 1 teaspoon of the sugar. Stir in 1 cup of the flour. Shape into a ball, cut a cross in the top, place it in a bowl, cover, and keep warm to rise until double in size.

Add the remaining sugar, flour, milk and salt. Mix well and knead until dough is smooth and elastic. Place dough in a greased bowl, grease the top of the dough, cover, and let rise in a warm place until it has doubled in size.

Roll the dough into a rectangle ½ inch thick. Wash the butter in cold water, working it well and pressing it in a clean cloth to remove excess water. Spread the butter over the dough and fold the dough into thirds, making three layers.

Roll dough out again and fold it into thirds. Wrap it in waxed paper and chill well, preferably overnight.

When ready to use, roll the dough out and fold the ends to the center. Roll and fold again twice more. Chill thoroughly, about 1 hour.

Divide dough in half and roll each half into a circle 1/8 inch thick. Cut each circle in 18 triangles or wedges. Starting at the wide end, roll the wedges of dough to the tip end, pressing to seal the end. Shape in crescents and place on greased baking sheets. Brush the beaten egg yolks over the tops of the crescents. Cover them with waxed paper and let them rise in a warm place until double in size. Bake in a preheated hot oven (400 degrees) 5 minutes. Reduce heat to 350 degrees and bake 15 minutes or until crescents are golden brown. Makes 36.

"Waverley found Miss Bradwardine presiding over the teas and coffee the table loaded with warm bread, both of flour, oatmeal and barley meal, in the shape of loaves, cakes, biscuits, and other varieties, together with eggs, reindeer ham, mutton and beef ditto, smoked salmon, marmalade, and all other delicacies which induced even Johnson himself to extol the luxury of Scotch breakfast above that of all other countries." Sir Walter Scott from *Waverley*

Diet Loaf

Sir Walter Scott (1771-1832) mentioned this very light sponge in his novel *St. Ronan's Well*. It is a traditional Scottish recipe and the word "diet" only means that it is a light loaf. The Scots would consume this at breakfast with a cup of tea.

- 1 pound granulated sugar
- 8 ounces soft butter
- 6 eggs
- Nearly 4 cups sifted all purpose flour
- ½ teaspoon cinnamon
- Finely grated peel of 1 lemon

Whisk the eggs thoroughly. Cream the butter and sugar to make it light and frothy and slowly beat in the whisked eggs. Add the lemon rind and cinnamon and then gradually beat in the flour, beating continually to ensure the mixture is kept light.

Line a large cake pan with greased paper and pour in the mixture.

Bake in a pre-heated oven at 375 degrees for 35 minutes until golden brown and well risen. You can sprinkle icing sugar (frosting) on top five minutes before removing from the oven. Allow to cool for ten minutes before removing from the cake pan. Cool on a wire rack. Some people add a layer of icing to the top once it is cold.

"Life ain't all beer and skittles (hush puppies), and more's the pity." George du
Maurier (1834-1896)
"Life is not wholly beer and skittles,
A treasure hunt for love and vittles."
Ogden Nash's spoof of du Maurier's quotation

Hush Puppies

Cajun entertainer and chef Justin Wilson (1914-2001) specializes in
Cajun and Creole cooking. He wrote several cookbooks including *Cajun
Fables, Justin Wilson Cookbook, Justin Wilson Gourmet and Gourmand
Cookbook, Outside Cooking With Inside Help.*

He said there was no way to estimate the number of hush puppies this
recipe will make because each person makes them a different size.

- 2 cups cornmeal
- 1 cup white flour
- ¼ teaspoon cayenne pepper
- 1 teaspoon baking powder
- ½ teaspoon soda
- 1 teaspoon salt
- ½ teaspoon garlic powder
- 2 eggs, beaten
- 1 cup buttermilk
- 1 cup green onion, finely chopped
- 2 tablespoons bacon drippings, hot
- ½ cup parsley, finely chopped
- Deep fat for frying

Combine all dry ingredients. Add eggs, buttermilk, onions, bacon drippings, parsley and stir well. Drop balls into hot fat and fry until golden brown. This will make 48, 47, 46 hush puppies.

"Marry Ann; and at the end of a week you'll find no more inspiration in her than in a plate of muffins." George Bernard Shaw (1856-1950)

Monticello Muffins

Thomas Jefferson (1743-1826) who helped write many famous American documents liked the muffin recipe of Peter Hemings, head cook at Monticello. He therefore instructed his daughter thusly. "Pray enable yourself to direct us here how to make muffins in Peter's method. My cook here cannot succeed at all in them, and they are a great luxury to me." This "Receipt for Monticello Muffins" was recorded in the manuscript cookbook of Jefferson's granddaughter.

Notes in parentheses may guide the modern reader in quantities and preparation.

"To a quart of flour (4 cups) put two table spoonfuls (1 ½ packets) of yeast. Mix the flour up with water (1 ½ cups) so thin that the dough will stick to the table. Our cook takes it up and throws it down until it will no longer stick. She puts it to rise until morning (covered with a towel in a warm place).

"In the morning she works the dough over the first thing and makes it into little cakes like biscuit (golf ball size) and sets them aside (an hour or so) until it is time to bake them. You know muffins are baked in a griddle in the hearth of the stove, not inside. (Cook on an ungreased griddle over medium heat for about 5 minutes on each side.) They bake very quickly.

"The second plate full is put on the fire when breakfast is sent in and they are ready by the time the first are eaten."

"The laziest man I ever met put popcorn in his pancakes so they would turn over themselves." W. C. Fields (1879-1946)

Pancakes With Milk

In the world's earliest cookbook, Apicius (1st century) wrote down this interesting recipe for pancakes with milk. This recipe is available on the Internet.

- 8 eggs
- 600 ml. of milk (2 ½ cups)
- 100 ml. of oil (slightly less than ½ cup)
- Honey
- Ground pepper

Mix eggs, milk and oil for the pancake dough. Fry and serve topped with honey and pepper.

"Bachelor's fare is bread and cheese and kisses." Jonathan Swift (1667-1745)

Parlies

"Parlies" or "Scottish Parliament Cakes" were small biscuits supplied to the gentry and Members of the Scottish Parliament by a shop in Waverley, Edinburgh. Sir Walter Scott (1771-1832) wrote the Waverley novels to pay off creditors but his stories of chivalry, patriotism and history brought esteem to Scotland.

In 1822, he was asked to preside over the welcome of an English king to Edinburgh for the first time in 171 years. He was given a Parlie along with the other members of Parliament on that eventful day.

- 8 ounces (2 ½ cups) all purpose flour
- 4 ounces butter or margarine
- 4 ounces brown sugar
- 1 egg
- 4 ounces or 2 tablespoons treacle (molasses)
- 2 teaspoons ground ginger

Mix the flour, ginger and sugar thoroughly. Melt the butter in a saucepan and add the treacle and bring to a boil, stirring continuously. Turn off the heat and add the other ingredients, mixing vigorously.

When cooled sufficiently to handle, scoop up a small quantity of the mixture with a teaspoon and push off with another teaspoon onto a well-greased baking tray or sheet. Flatten slightly with a fork and leave space between each one to allow it to spread. Cook at 325 degrees for 25-30 minutes.

Lift biscuits off the tray and store in an airtight container until serving time.

"Here is bread, which strengthens man's heart, and therefore called the staff of life." Matthew Henry (1662-1714)

Pizza Bread

Sophia Loren, Italian actress of many movies, has written a cookbook called *Sophia Loren's Recipes and Memories* and other books such as *Living and Loving.*

Some of her most famous movies were *Two Women, Heller in Pink Tights, Marriage Italian Style, Yesterday Today and Tomorrow, Houseboat, Gold of Naples, El Cid, A Countess From Hong Kong* and many others.

This recipe from her book is available on the Internet.

- 1 package roll mix or pizza mix
- ½ cup yellow corn meal
- Olive oil
- Your favorite toppings and spices

Follow the directions on the box of any packaged roll or pizza mix. When the dough has risen, knead into it as much yellow corn meal as it will take. Grease your pizza pan, cookie sheet, or large pie pan with olive or vegetable oil. Roll out the dough to ¼" thickness and press into the pan. Pour more oil on the top and spread it over the surface of the dough.

Add the goodies to your own taste: Anchovies, Cheese, Olives, Tomato sauce, Pizza sauce, Sausage, Mushrooms and spices such as Marjoram, Rosemary, Thyme and Oregano. Bake 15-20 minutes at 425 degrees. Cut into wedges.

"I think you will be happy with my one secret: Yellow corn meal in the dough."

Remuda Ranch Beer Biscuits

Sophie Burden, radio personality and dude ranch hostess in Wickenburg Arizona, (the World's Dude Ranch Capital) wrote a regular newspaper column. In it, she described this method of making beer biscuits for dude ranch guests in the 1920s.

Sophie used beer instead of milk in her biscuits. She said, "The main thing is to work the dough out just as little as possible. It doesn't matter if it's old stale beer because it's the malt that adds the good flavor. The alcohol cooks out, much to the disgust of certain teenagers."

Sophie would choose about as much Bisquick as she thought would be right for the number of people, then mix in the beer till it was about the consistency of baking powder biscuits. Then she'd flop it all on a board and pat it out to about ¼ inch thick. Then she would cut them out to whatever size she wanted.

She'd butter up the baking pan, flop the biscuits in, brush melted butter on top, and bake them 15 minutes at 475.

Sometimes she would add grated cheese to the dough or chopped onion, chopped cooked bacon or sausage. Whatever she thought would taste good.

Chapter 9

DESSERTS

Washing the Dishes

When we on simple rations sup
How easy is the washing up!
But heavy feeding complicates
The task by soiling many plates.

And though I grant that I have prayed
That we might find a serving-maid,
I'd scullion all my days I think,
To see her smile across the sink!

I wash, she wipes. In water hot
I souse each pan and dish and pot;
While Taffy mutters, purrs, and begs,
And rubs himself against my legs.

The man who never in his life
Has washed the dishes with his wife
Or polished up the silver plate
He still is largely celibate.

One warning: There is certain ware
That must be handled with all care:
The Lord Himself will give you up
If you should drop a willow cup!
Christopher Morley (1890-1957)

"I do not as a rule seek advice about food from thin people." Jeffry Steingarten

Almond Tartlets

Edmond Rostand (1868-1918) wrote the famous love story of *Cyrano de Bergerac.* In the second act called "The Poet's Eating House," Cyrano's friend is trying to divert people from the hero by tantalizing them with a recipe told in a poem.

"Beat your eggs up, light and quick,
Froth them thick;
Mingle with them while you beat
Juice of lemon,
Essence fine;
Then combine
The burst milk of almonds sweet.
Circle with a custard paste
The slim waist
Of your tartlet molds;
Then top with a skillful finger print
Nick and dint,
Round their edge then drop by drop
In its dainty bed
Your cream shed:
In the oven place each mold:
Reappearing softly browned,
The renowned
Almond tartlets you behold."

"Though I look old, yet I am strong and lusty; for in my youth I never did apply hot and rebellious liquors in my blood." William Shakespeare (1564-1619)

Almost As Good As Sex Cheesecake

Dr. Ruth Westheimer is known for her explicit writings and views on sex. She has written *Dr. Ruth's Encyclopedia of Sex, Sex For Dummies, Heavenly Sex: Sexuality in the Jewish Tradition,* as well as many columns giving sexual advice. Despite her petite frame, she enjoys fine cuisine as her cheesecake recipe shows. This recipe is available on the Internet.

- 5 ounces graham cracker crumbs
- 3 tablespoons sugar
- 5 tablespoons butter, melted
- 16 ounces cream cheese, soft
- ½ cup sugar
- 1 pinch of salt
- 2 large eggs
- 3 tablespoons Chambord (raspberry) liqueur
- 8 ounces sour cream
- 1 tablespoon sugar
- ½ teaspoon vanilla
- 1 tablespoon Chambord liqueur
- 1 cup raspberries, fresh

Preheat oven to 350 degrees. To make the crust, mix cracker crumbs, sugar and butter. Press the mixture into bottom of 9" spring form pan.

To make the filling, mix cream cheese, sugar, vanilla and salt at medium speed with electric mixer. Add eggs and mix until well blended. Fold 3 tablespoons Chambord into batter. Pour the mixture into the crust. Bake approximately 40 minutes or until golden brown. Loosen the cake from the rim of the pan. Let it cool and remove the rim of the pan.

To make the topping, mix sour cream, sugar, vanilla, and 1 tablespoon Chambord and spread evenly over the cheesecake. Refrigerate for 4 hours or until firm. Top with fresh raspberries just before serving. Serves 8.

"The admiral says that he never beheld so fair a thing: trees all along the river, beautiful and green, and different from ours, with flowers and fruits each according to their kind." Christopher Columbus (1451-1506) in 1492 upon arriving in the New World

Apricot Compote

Alexander Dumas (1802-1870) wrote many adventure stories in addition to his cookbook and famous recipes. In the *Count of Monte Cristo*, Dumas described how to build up immunity over 20 days to a poison so that one may toast the enemy with the very lemonade that will kill him.

There is nothing fatal about this recipe except the ecstasy, which results from eating it. The recipe is available on the Internet.

- ½ cup water
- 1 cup sugar
- 8 ounces apricot halves, fresh
- 1 orange juiced or 8 tablespoons juice

Halve and pit the apricots. In a heavy, medium saucepan, boil the water and sugar until thickened into syrup, about 5 minutes. Add the apricots to the hot syrup and cook over medium heat for 3 minutes.

Remove from heat and add the orange juice. Let it cool before serving. Serves 4 alone, over ice cream or over simple cake like pound cake.

"Would ye both eat your cake and have your cake?" John Heywood (1497-1580)

Baba au Rhum

Isak Dinesen, pen name of Karen Blixen (1885-1962), wrote *Babette's Feast* which was made into a French movie. Many have tried to create dishes from this haunting story and movie.

This recipe was modeled after the description in the book and the movie and comparisons to the usual French recipes for this dessert.

- 1 cake fresh yeast
- 1/3 cup warm milk
- 2 1/3 cups sifted flour
- 8 tablespoons unsalted butter, soft
- 2 2/3 cups sugar
- 6 eggs
- 5 ½ cups water
- ½ cup dark rum
- Candied fruits for decoration

Dissolve yeast in milk in a large bowl. Stir in ½ cup of the flour. Cover and set aside in a warm place to rise for 30 minutes.

Beat 7 tablespoons of the butter in an electric mixer or in a food proces-sor. Beat in 2 tablespoons of the sugar and 2 tablespoons of the flour. Beat in eggs one at a time.

Beat remaining flour into the risen yeast mixture, then beat in the but-ter and egg mixture to make a thick, doughlike batter. Butter a large baba or Savarin mold or a bundt pan with the remaining tablespoon of butter and spoon batter into the mold. It should fill it halfway. Cover with a clean cloth and set aside to rise until dough reaches the top of the mold.

Preheat oven to 350 degrees. Bake baba for about 40 minutes, until nicely browned on top. While baking, combine remaining sugar with water in a saucepan and boil until syrupy and reduced to 3 cups. Remove from heat and stir in rum. When baba is baked, remove it from oven and carefully spoon warm rum syrup over it, allowing it to saturate the cake completely.

Cool completely, unmold and decorate with candied cherries or fruits before serving. Serves 8 to 12.

"Nose, nose, nose, nose!
And who gave thee this jolly nose?
Nutmegs and ginger, cinnamon and clove,
And they gave me this jolly red nose."
Thomas Ravenscroft (1590-1633)

Black Cake

Emily Dickinson (1830-1886) in addition to being an outstanding poet was quite a cook. She rarely left her house and entertained little but sent her poems and recipes to friends. This black cake recipe is actually more like a fruitcake and has unusual directions, which are not typographical errors.

Just as with fruitcake, the longer it sits in a cool place, the better it tastes. Emily used to keep hers in the cellar for a month or so. This recipe is available on the Internet.

- 2 cups sugar
- ½ pound butter
- 5 eggs
- ¼ cup molasses
- 2 cups sifted flour
- ½ teaspoon baking soda
- 1 teaspoon cloves
- 1 teaspoon mace
- 1 teaspoon cinnamon
- ½ nutmeg, ground
- ¼ to ½ cup brandy
- 1 pound raisins
- 2/3 pound currants
- 2/3 pound citron

Add the sugar to butter gradually and mix until light and creamy. Add the eggs and molasses and beat well. Resift flour with soda and spices. If you are using unsalted butter, add ½ teaspoon of salt. Beat sifted ingredients into mixture, adding brandy gradually.

Stir in raisins, currants and citron. (Note: smaller amounts of raisins, currants and citron will suffice, if desired.)

Place a pan of water in the oven while heating the oven to 225 degrees. Pour batter into two loaf pans lined with waxed paper or aluminum foil.

Bake at 225 degrees for *3 hours*, keeping the pan of water at least 1 inch full to add moisture.

Remove the pan of water for the last half hour. Let loaves cool before removing from pans. Wrap in fresh foil or waxed paper after cooling for storage. Serves 16 or more.

"It is the destiny of mint to be crushed." Waverley Root

Blancmange with Brandied Apricots

This dessert was such a favorite with Thomas Jefferson (1743-1826) that he had several recipes in his Monticello cookbook.

Jefferson, who wrote most of *The Declaration of Independence* and other works, was a frequent visitor to France. This version of his favorite dessert may have been one that he brought back from there. This recipe is available on the Internet.

- 2 cups whole almonds, blanched
- 2 cups whole milk
- 1 teaspoon pure almond extract
- 2 ½ teaspoons unflavored gelatin
- ¾ cup granulated white sugar
- 1 cup chilled heavy cream
- 1 recipe brandied apricots
- Crushed mint leaves or toasted sliced almonds

Lightly oil or spray eight ½ cup decorative molds. Spread almonds in a 12-inch skillet and toast until pale golden (not dark), 7-8 minutes. Cool almonds before proceeding. Process the toasted almonds with the milk in a food processor 1-2 minutes until thick but not completely pureed. Wring out the almond milk from the ground almonds using a piece of doubled cheesecloth.

Rinse a doubled 18-inch long piece of cheesecloth in cold water and wring it out. Line a large sieve with the cheesecloth and set over a bowl. Pour the milk mixture into the cheesecloth and carefully squeeze the almond milk (about 1 cup) from the cloth through the sieve and into the bowl, discarding both the almonds and the cloth. Stir in the extract.

In a small bowl, sprinkle the gelatin over 2 ½ tablespoons cold water and let it stand 1 minute to dissolve. Meanwhile, combine almond milk and sugar in a small saucepan and cook over moderate heat, stirring, until the sugar is dissolved. Pour the almond mixture into a bowl set in a larger bowl of ice water and cool, stirring constantly, until it starts to get thick and gelatinous. Reserve at room temperature.

Beat the cream until it holds stiff peaks and whisk one quarter into the almond mixture to lighten it. Fold in the remaining whipped cream gently but thoroughly using a flexible spatula, and spoon the mixture in the prepared dishes. Chill the blancmanges, covered with plastic wrap, until set.

Brandied Apricot Recipe prepared days or weeks in advance:
- 2 pounds canned apricot halves in syrup
- 1 whole clove
- 1 small stick of cinnamon
- ½ cup white sugar
- Apricot brandy
- 3 drops almond extract

Drain the apricot halves and reserve both the fruit and the syrup, placing the apricots into quart jars. Pour the syrup into a saucepan, add the sugar, clove and cinnamon. Boil until the syrup has reduced by half. Let cool to room temperature, strain, and measure the amount of syrup you have. Add an equal amount of apricot brandy to the cooled syrup, along with the almond extract. Pour the brandied syrup over the apricots in the jars. Cover and refrigerate for several days since they improve with age.

To serve, unmold each blancmange by dipping the dish in hot water for an instant, and turn onto a dessert plate. Surround it with brandied apricots, some crushed mint leaves and some sliced toasted almonds. Serves 8.

"A gourmet who thinks of calories is like a tart who looks at her watch." James A. Beard (1903-1985)

Boccone Dolce (Sweet Mouthful)

Vincent (1911-1993) and Mary Price, in their book *A Treasury of Great Recipes* outdid themselves with this Italian combination of strawberries and chocolate in meringue. Everyone who has tried this recipe has raves for it. The recipe is available on the Internet.

First make meringue layers:
- 4 egg whites, room temperature
- ¼ teaspoon salt
- ¼ teaspoon cream of tartar
- 1 teaspoon cider vinegar
- 1 cup superfine sugar

Preheat oven to 275 degrees. In mixer, beat egg whites, salt, tartar, vinegar and extract until soft peaks form. Gradually beat in sugar until meringue is stiff and glossy.

Line baking sheets with parchment or waxed paper. Trace three 8-inch circles on paper. Spread meringue evenly and equally over circles. Bake one hour or until meringue becomes bisque colored. Then turn off oven, open oven door, and let meringues "rest" in oven another 15 minutes.

Remove from oven and carefully peel parchment/paper off meringue. Put meringue on racks to dry until thoroughly cool. Once cooled, meringues may be wrapped in saran and frozen.

Wrap each meringue in several saran layers, then stack gently in a large plastic container for freezing. Remove from freezer at least an hour before assembling.

Then make strawberry chocolate filling for meringue layers.
- 6 ounces semi-sweet chocolate pieces
- 3 tablespoons water
- 3 tablespoons powdered sugar
- 3 cups heavy cream
- ½ teaspoon vanilla extract
- 1 pint fresh strawberries, sliced
- 1 pint strawberries, sliced; sugared
- Chocolate curls for garnish

Melt the chocolate pieces and 3 tablespoons water in a double boiler over hot water. Stir until smooth and remove from heat. Cool but don't let it harden.

In a large bowl, whip the cream until stiff; gradually adding powdered sugar and then vanilla extract.

Slice two pints of strawberries. One is used between meringue layers; the other is sliced, sugared and refrigerated to produce more juice. The sugared berries are served as a sauce. Save several whole berries for garnish.

To assemble, place a meringue layer on a serving plate, rounded side down. Spread a VERY THIN coating of chocolate over it. GO EASY on chocolate. Too much will make it impossible to cut the cake.

Top chocolate with a layer (3/4 inch thick) of whipped cream. Top cream with a layer of sliced berries. Place a second layer of meringue on top of this and repeat the filling. Top with final meringue, rounded side up, and frost sides and top smoothly with remaining whipped cream. Additional cream may be used to pipe a design onto sides and top of cake. Refrigerate at least four hours or overnight. Garnish with whole strawberries and chocolate curls. Serves 8.

"If the people have no bread, let them eat cake." Marie Antoinette

Cake

This cake was a personal recipe of Marie Antoinette (1755-1793) written in her own hand in French. It was not the kind of cake she meant in her famous quotation above. In her actual quotation, she said that the people without bread should eat "brioche" which is a spongey sort of bun. Marie was quite aware that French royalty was being accused of extravagance and she was cutting back on household staff and eliminating positions based on privilege. But it was not enough.

Marie, Queen of France, lost her husband, Louis XVI, to the guillotine during the French Revolution in 1793 and nine months later she suffered the same fate.

This cake recipe was popular because it contained the new exotic delight called chocolate. A French physician said that cacao would be addictive, and many would agree with him.

- 48 ladyfingers
- ¾ cup heavy cream
- 6 ripe peaches
- 1 teaspoon lemon zest
- ¾ cup espresso
- ¼ cup Grand Marnier liqueur
- 2 ounces white chocolate
- 1 ounce bittersweet chocolate
- 6 tablespoons light brown sugar
- 24 ounces Mascarpone cheese (Italian only)

Combine cooled espresso, 2 tablespoons brown sugar and Grand Marnier. Peel peaches, slice and combine with lemon zest and 2 tablespoons more of brown sugar. Set aside.

Grate white chocolate and keep cold. Whip cream until soft peaks form. Fold in 2 tablespoons brown sugar and fold in room temperature Mascarpone.

Dip some of the ladyfingers into the espresso mixture and line bottom of a 10 inch springform pan. Next line the sides of the pan with unsoaked ladyfingers in a standing pattern to create a fence. Sprinkle ½ of the white chocolate over the ladyfingers. Spread ½ of the Mascarpone mixture and then cover it with 1/3 of the peaches.

Repeat the process with more dipped ladyfingers, the other ½ of the white chocolate, ½ of the Mascarpone and another 1/3 of the peaches. Then top with grated bittersweet chocolate and lay the rest of the peaches in a decorative pattern on top of the dessert.

Leave in the refrigerator for 8 to 24 hours before serving.

"Knew a bloke once called Damper Dan
Remember the bludger well I can
And his dampers.
Bottomless moleskins hangin' slack
Tin of treacle, sticky and black,
Heap of flour in a dirty sack
For dampers.
Beef or mutton he wouldn't touch
Brownie or cake he didn't like much,
Only damper.
'Nothin,' he'd say, 'like good clean flour
Never gets stale or moldy or sour
Nothin' gives yer muscular power
Like damper."
Keith Garvey

Damper

Daniel Bowen, an Australian humorous writer, penned such unforgettable titles as *How to Destroy Your Video, Great Vomits of the Twentieth Century, Diary of an Average Australian* and *Toxic Custard Guide to Australia.* In the latter, he described how to make Damper, a dish prepared in the outback by bushmen who had little more than a fire and the most basic of ingredients. This recipe is available on the Internet. His delightful cooking directions are quoted verbatim.

- 3 cups self-raising flour
- 1-2 teaspoons of salt
- 3.2 ounces of melted butter
- ½ cup water
- ½ cup milk

- More milk for glazing
- More flour for dusting
- Extra butter for serving
- Golden syrup or honey

"Rev up the oven to 210 degrees C (for you imperial people that's 410 degrees F.) Brush an oven tray with melted butter or oil (cooking oil that is, not Castrol GTX.) Sift flour and salt into a large mixing bowl, and make a well in the middle. If you've got time, pause for a quick singalong of 'Jack and Jill.'

"Stir up the butter, water and milk, and add to the flour. Stir it with a knife until just combined.

"Throw it out of the bowl onto a flour surface and knead it for 20 seconds (that's 20.5 seconds imperial) or until it's smooth. Then plonk it into a tray and use your sculpture skills to make it into a round shape about 20 centimetres (about 7.874 inches, stop me if I'm getting too precise) across.

"Use a sharp pointed knife (Stanley knife not recommended), score it into 8 sections (8), about 1 centimetre deep (0.39 inches.) Brush it with milk and dust it with flour, then throw it in the oven for 10 minutes.

"Reduce the heat to 180 C (356 F) and continue to bake for about 15 minutes or until it's golden and sounds hollow when tapped. Serve with loads of butter and/or syrup and/or honey. Even cream and jam is nice too."

"A spoonful of honey will catch more flies than a gallon of vinegar." Benjamin Franklin (1706-1790)

Dates in Saffron

Kitab al-Tabikh, written in an eighth century Baghdad cookbook, created by a member of a royal family and a female slave in Islam's earliest culinary text. Source: Stewart Lee Allen's *In the Devil's Garden.*

- 1 pound fresh dates
- Blanched almonds, one per date
- 3 tablespoons rosewater
- ¼ teaspoon saffron
- 2 tablespoons honey
- 2 tablespoons sugar, plus more to cover
- 2 teaspoons cinnamon

Slice and replace each date pit with one blanched almond. Close up the little date. Simmer the rosewater, saffron and honey for a few minutes. Let it cool and pour the concoction over the dates covering them all. Mix the cinnamon and sugar together. Take the dates from their concoction and roll them in the sugar/cinnamon.

For added flavor, cover them with more sugar. Keep the dates in your wine cellar or refrigerator. Serve them to your hot sheik slightly cool.

"Food is an important part of a balanced diet." Fran Lebowitz

Dear Abby's Pecan Pie

Abigail Van Buren (the pen name for Pauline Phillips and her daughter, Jeanne Phillips) wrote syndicated newspaper columns giving practical advice for years. This recipe drew rave reviews from readers and had to be republished several times in her column. The recipe is available on the Internet.

- 1 cup white corn syrup
- 1 cup dark brown sugar, firmly packed

- 1/3 teaspoon salt
- 1/3 cup melted butter
- 1 teaspoon vanilla
- 3 eggs slightly beaten
- 1 9" unbaked pie shell
- 1 cup whole pecans

Preheat oven to 350 degrees. Mix syrup, sugar, salt, butter and vanilla. Add eggs. Mix and pour into shell. Sprinkle pecans over the filling. Bake 45 minutes or longer if an electric oven is used. Serves 6.

"Well, if I called the wrong number, why did you answer the phone?" James Thurber

Devil's Food Cake

James Thurber (1894-1961) was a cartoonist and author who wrote and drew for The New Yorker and other publications. He wrote Fables for Our Time, The Thurber Carnival, My Life and Hard Times and other things. His *The Secret Life of Walter Mitty* was made into a movie with Danny Kaye playing the introvert who dreamed of adventure and love.

Thurber's wife wrote down many recipes that have been passed down through the family. This one is available on the Internet and is called "Mame Thurber's Never-Fail Devil's Food Cake." The icing was called "Mame's $100 Chocolate Frosting," because of a contest she won.

- 1 cup light brown sugar
- ½ cup unsweetened chocolate, finely grated

- ½ cup milk
- 1 egg yolk

Combine and cook these ingredients together over low heat until mixture is smooth. Cool slightly while mixing other ingredients.

- ½ cup butter
- 1 cup light brown sugar
- 2 eggs, separated
- ½ cup milk
- 2 ½ cups sifted cake flour
- ¼ teaspoon baking powder
- ½ teaspoon salt
- 1 teaspoon vanilla
- 1 teaspoon soda

Preheat the oven to 350 degrees. Cream together the butter and sugar. Beat in yolks. Add milk alternately with sifted flour, baking powder, baking soda, and salt. Stir in cooled chocolate mixture and vanilla. Gently fold in stiffly beaten egg whites. Pour into two greased 8 inch cake pans. Bake for 30-35 minutes, or until done.

Let cakes cool. If the tops are uneven, scalp with a knife before frosting.

Frosting:
- ¼ pound butter
- 1 square unsweetened chocolate, melted
- 2/3 pound confectioner's sugar
- 1 egg
- 1 teaspoon vanilla

- 1 teaspoon lemon juice
- ½ cup chopped nuts

Melt butter; cool. Add, with melted chocolate and sugar, to beaten egg. Stir in vanilla and lemon juice. Beat until smooth. Fold in nuts. Frosts one 8 inch layer cake.

"Sir Toby: Dost thou think, because thou art virtuous, there shall be no more cakes and ale?
Clown: Yes, by Saint Ann; and ginger shall be hot I' the mouth." William Shakespeare (1564-1619)

Gingerbread

Vincent Price (1911-1993), art connoisseur and actor, wrote a cookbook with his wife, Mary, called *A Treasury of Great Recipes*. This rather spicy gingerbread might be a bit too wild for children but adults love it. This recipe is available on the Internet.

- ½ cup butter
- 1 cup sugar
- 1 egg
- 1 tablespoon corn syrup
- 1 tablespoon molasses
- 2 cups flour
- ½ teaspoon salt
- 2 teaspoons ginger
- 1 teaspoon baking soda

- ¾ cup boiling water
- 2-4 tablespoons chopped crystallized ginger

Cream butter and sugar and beat in egg, corn syrup and molasses. Mix salt, ginger and flour. Mix baking soda with water. Add flour mixture alternately to creamed mixture with water and soda. Stir in crystallized ginger. Bake in a greased round 8-inch pan at 350 degrees for 25-30 minutes. Turn out on a rack to cool, but it's best served warm, especially with whipped cream or lemon curd.

"I doubt the world holds for anyone a more soul-stirring surprise than the first adventure with ice cream." Heywood Broun (1888-1939)

Ice Cream

Thomas Jefferson (1743-1826) traveled to Europe and brought back many recipes. In addition, he had a garden and grew every kind of vegetable and herb, as well as cultivating plants brought back by Lewis and Clark from their expedition. He wrote out this recipe for ice cream in 1815.

He had an icehouse at Monticello to preserve meat and butter, to chill wine and to make ice cream. Visitors noted that Jefferson's ice cream was served as balls inside of warm pastry. This recipe is in the *Jefferson Papers* collection at the Library of Congress.

- 2 bottles of good cream (1 quart)
- 6 yolks of eggs
- ½ pound of sugar (1 cup)

"Mix the yolks & sugar. Put the cream on a fire in a casserole, first putting in a stick of Vanilla. When near boiling take it off & pour it gently into the mixture of eggs & sugar. Stir it well. Put it on the fire again stirring it thoroughly with a spoon to prevent its sticking to the casserole. When near boiling take it off and strain it thro a towel. Put it in the Sabottiere* then set it in ice an hour before it is to be served. Put into the ice a handful of salt. Put salt on the coverlid of the Sabottiere & cover the whole with ice. Leave it still half a quarter of an hour. Then turn the Sabottiere in the ice 10 minutes. Open it to loosen with a spatula the ice from the inner sides of the Sabottiere. Shut it and replace it in the ice. Open it from time to time to detach the ice from the sides. When well taken, stir it well with the Spatula. Put it in moulds, jostling it well down on the knee. Then put the mould into the same bucket of ice. Leave it there to the moment of serving it. To withdraw it, immerse the mould in warm water, turning it well till it will come out & turn it into a plate."

*The sabottiere is the inner container of the ice cream maker. There was no crank to turn it. When Jefferson wrote about turning the Sabottiere in the ice 10 minutes, he meant for someone to grab the handle and turn the canister clockwise and then counterclockwise.

"Adam was but human, this explains it all. He did not want the apple for the apple's sake, he only wanted it because it was forbidden." Mark Twain (1835-1910)

Incredible Oedipal Pie

Austrian neurologist Sigmund Freud (1856-1939) invented psychoanalysis in the process of listening to and trying to understand patients and their psychological problems. He wrote of the love of boys for their mothers and their wish to replace their father in their mother's eyes. He called it the Oedipus Complex after the Greek tragedy in which Oedipus killed his father and married his mother. He wrote *The Interpretation of Dreams, Totem and Taboo, Psychoanalysis,* and many other standard psychological texts.

James Hillman (author of *The Dream and the Underworld* and *The Myth of Analysis)* and Charles Boer (translator of *Homeric Hymns* and *Book of Life*) wrote a humorous cookbook called *Freud's Cookbook,* which included this recipe for "Incredible Oedipal Pie," a takeoff on "Mom's Apple Pie." Freud is supposedly writing this recipe.

- 1 cup sugar
- 2 tablespoons flour
- Dash of salt
- 4-5 sliced apples, peeled and cored
- ½ cup raisins
- ½ cup chopped walnuts
- 3 tablespoons dark rum
- ¼ cup butter melted
- Pie crust

Make this pie while thinking of your mother. In fact, it is best if you make it while she is watching you and you can ask for her favorite piecrust recipe. Line a pie pan with this crust. Add the apple mixture and cover with crust. Bake at 450 degrees for 10 minutes, then reduce the temperature to 350 and bake 25 minutes more. Cool to room temperature.

It's okay to give your mother a piece because these days they call it "Mom's Apple Pie." But in 1897, I remember, "crying my heart out, because my mother was nowhere to be found." Then I soon recognized that the "love of mother and jealousy of the father was a general phenomenon of early childhood." So dad gets none of this pie.

"Great with child and longing for stewed prunes." William Shakespeare (1564-1619)

Kaiserschmarrn or Emperor's Trifle

Dr. Edith Buxbaum (1902-1982), Viennese child psychoanalyst who studied with Anna Freud (Sigmund's daughter), helped found the Seattle Psychoanalytic Institute. She also wrote *Your Child Makes Sense* and *Troubled Children in a Troubled World*. She called this old Viennese recipe "junk fit for a king. It is usually served with a raspberry or prune jam. See details below."

- 1/3 cup shortening or oil
- 2/3 cup flour
- 1/3 cup sugar
- 6 eggs, separated
- ½ cup plus 2 tablespoons water
- 4 tablespoons melted butter
- 2/3 cup raisins
- 2-3 tablespoons additional sugar

Melt the shortening in a large metal cake pan or skillet set over medium heat. Plump the raisins for 10 minutes in boiling water and then drain them.

Start heating the oven at 400 degrees. Mix the flour and water in a large bowl. In a separate small bowl add water to egg yolks and combine well. Pour the egg mixture into the dry ingredients, mixing well with a whisk.

Beat egg whites stiff, then fold them gently into the liquid mixture. Pour into the heated pan with the fat. Remove from heat at once and place in the oven. Bake until golden brown (8-10 minutes); then put back on stove top.

Tear into 2-3 inch squares, using two forks. Drizzle melted butter over, then sprinkle with raisins and sugar.

Serve with raspberry syrup or prune jam. To make prune jam (or Zwetschkenroster), cook dried prunes with water and sugar in a saucepan until it becomes a not so thick jam. Then add cinnamon and cloves to use as a topping on this trifle. Serves 8.

"The fly that sips treacle is lost in the sweets,
So he that tastes woman, woman, woman,
He that tastes woman, ruin meets."
John Gay (1688-1732)

Laura's Gingerbread

Laura Ingalls Wilder (1867-1957) wrote the Little House series of stories that was made into the television series, *Little House on the Prairie,* some 17 years after her death. In 1953, she sent this gingerbread recipe to Jennie Lindquist who was preparing a Christmas book.

- 1 cup brown sugar
- ½ cup lard or other shortening.
- 1 cup treacle (molasses)
- 2 teaspoons baking soda
- 3 cups flour
- 1 teaspoon ginger
- 1 teaspoon cinnamon

- 1 teaspoon allspice
- 1 teaspoon nutmeg
- 1 teaspoon cloves
- ½ teaspoon salt
- 2 eggs

Blend the sugar with the shortening. Add the molasses and mix well. Put baking soda in 1 cup of boiling water. (Be sure cup is full of water after foam is run off into cake mixture.) Mix all well.

To the flour, add the spices and salt. Sift all into the cake mixture and mix well. Add lastly 2 well-beaten eggs. The mixture should be quite thin. Bake in a moderate oven (325-350 degrees) for 30 minutes. Raisins and, or, candied fruit may be added and a chocolate frosting adds to the goodness.

"There is something about a martini,
Ere the dining and dancing begin,
And to tell you the truth, it is not the vermouth.
I think that perhaps it's the gin".
Ogden Nash (1902-1971)

Lime Ice

This recipe for Lime Ice by Ernest Hemingway (1899-1961) is contained in *The Hemingway Cookbook* by David Boreth. The recipe is available on the Internet.

- 1 ½ cups sugar syrup
- Juice of 6 limes

- ½ tablespoon lemon juice
- 1 cup water
- 1 egg white
- 3 ½ tablespoons gin
- 2 tablespoons crème de menthe
- Rind of ½ lime, very finely chopped (optional)

To make the sugar syrup, dissolve 1 ¼ cups sugar in 1 cup water. This may be done by stirring the sugar into the water either at room temperature or over low heat. If done over heat, allow the syrup to cool completely before proceeding.

Remove the rind of half of 1 lime and cover with plastic wrap. Combine the juice of the 6 limes, lemon juice, sugar syrup, water and egg white in a large-bottomed, sturdy plastic container, so that the liquid is no more than 2 inches deep. Stir the mixture completely. Cover and place in the freezer for 1 ½-2 hours.

When ice has formed around the edge of the mixture and the center is slushy, blend for a few seconds with a hand mixer or whisk. Cover and return to the freezer for another 1 ½ hours or so. Repeat process, adding the gin, crème de menthe, and minced lime rind after the third freezing.

Return the mixture to the freezer for another 30-60 minutes, or until firmly frozen. The ice may be served directly from the freezer, as it will stay somewhat soft and scoopable from the alcohol included.

"If any man has drunk a little too deeply from the cup of physical pleasure; if he has spent too much time at his desk that should have been spent asleep; if his fine spirits have become temporarily dulled; if he finds the air too damp, the minutes too slow, and the atmosphere too heavy to withstand; if he is obsessed by a fixed idea which bars him from any freedom of thought: if he is any of these poor creatures, we say let him be given a good pint of amber-flavored chocolate...and marvels will be performed." Anthelme Brillat-Savarin (1755-1826)

Mississippi Mud Cake

Lillian Hellman wrote *The Little Foxes, Watch on the Rhine*, and other works. She was also the lover and final caretaker of Dashiell Hammett who wrote the Thin Man and Sam Spade series of mystery novels. Toward the end of her life, she wrote a cookbook called *Cooking Together*. This recipe, from that book, is available on the Internet.

- ½ cup bourbon
- 1 ½ cup coffee
- 5 ounces unsweetened chocolate
- 2 cups sugar
- Pinch salt
- 2 cups flour
- 1 teaspoon baking soda
- ¾ teaspoon baking powder
- 5 eggs
- 2 tablespoons vanilla

Preheat oven to 275 degrees. Melt chocolate in bourbon and coffee. Add sugar and salt. Combine flour, baking soda, and baking powder and gradually beat them into the chocolate mix. Do not overbeat. Lightly mix eggs and vanilla into the batter. Pour into a buttered and floured tub pan and bake for about 1 ½ hours.

The cake is done when a toothpick can be inserted without being coated with batter.

"Orange bright,
Like golden lamps in a green light."
Andrew Marvell (1621-1678)

Orange Marmalade Layer Cake

Jan Karon writes like a female Garrison Keillor. She wrote *A Common Life: The Wedding Story*. She described Esther Bolick's cake that put Father Tim Cavanagh into a diabetic coma just before he married Cynthia in Mitford, North Carolina.

Jan went to a Southern pastry chef (Scott Peacock) and asked him to create a "light, moist and seductive" recipe for the cake.

- 3 cups cake flour
- ½ teaspoon baking soda
- ½ teaspoon salt
- 1 cup (2 sticks) softened unsalted butter
- 2 cups granulated sugar
- 3 large eggs at room temperature, beaten lightly
- 1 tablespoon grated orange zest
- 1 ½ teaspoon vanilla
- 1 cup buttermilk, at room temperature

1. For the orange syrup, have 1 cup freshly squeezed orange juice and ½ cup sugar.

2. For the filling, have 1 cup orange marmalade. For the frosting, have ¾ cup well-chilled heavy cream, 3 tablespoons sugar and ¾ cup well-chilled sour cream.

3. Preheat the oven to 325 degrees. Butter two 9-inch round cake pans, lined with parchment or waxed paper, and butter and flour the paper, shaking out the excess.

4. In a bowl, sift the flour, baking soda and salt.

5. In a bowl with an electric mixer, beat the butter until combined, add the sugar, a little at a time, and beat the mixture until light and fluffy. Beat in the eggs, orange zest, and vanilla.

Beat in 1/3 of the dry ingredients alternately with ½ of the buttermilk until combined well. Add half the remaining dry ingredients and the remaining buttermilk. Beat until combined well. Beat the remaining dry ingredients until mixture is smooth.

Evenly divide the batter between the pans, smooth the surface, rap each part on the counter to expel any air pockets or bubbles, then transfer to the oven. Bake for 45 minutes or until a cake tester inserted in the middle comes out clean. Transfer to racks and cook in the pans for 20 minutes.

To make the orange syrup: In a bowl, stir the juice and sugar until sugar is dissolved. With a toothpick or wooden skewer, poke holes at ½ inch intervals in the cake layers and spoon the syrup over each layer, allowing the syrup to be completely absorbed before adding the remaining. Let layers cool completely.

To make the filling: In a small saucepan, set over moderate heat. Heat the marmalade until just melted. Let cool 5 minutes.

To make the frosting: In a bowl, whisk the heavy cream with the sugar until it forms firm peaks. Add the sour cream, a little at a time, and whisk until it will spread easily.

To assemble the cake: Arrange one of the layers on a cake plate. Carefully peel off the waxed paper. Then spread 2/3 of the marmalade over the top, smoothing it into an even layer. Invert the remaining layer onto the top of the first layer, peel off the waxed paper and spoon the remaining marmalade onto the center of it, leaving a 1 ¼ inch border around the edge. Frost the sides and top of the border with the frosting, leaving the marmalade on top of the cake exposed. Or if you prefer, frost the entire cake, adding the marmalade as a garnish on top. Chill at least 2 hours before serving.

"The ripest peach is highest on the tree." James Whitcomb Riley (1849-1916)

Peach Tart With Brandy Sauce

Thomas Jefferson (1743-1826) once said, "We abound in the luxury of the peach." He enjoyed surprising guests with bold new recipes he brought back from France or picked up from Indians during the Lewis and Clark expedition.

Peach brandy was as common a drink as apple cider during Jefferson's presidency. This recipe is available on the Internet.

- 1 cup sliced almonds
- 1 cup all purpose flour
- 2/3 cup butter
- 2 tablespoons brown sugar
- 1 tube almond paste sliced
- 2/3 cup softened butter
- 3 large eggs

- 8 peaches, cut into wedges
- Brandy sauce (below)

Process almonds in a food grinder until finely ground. Add flour, 2/3 cup butter and sugars. Mix and press into the bottom and sides of an 11 inch tart pan. Chill one hour. Line crust with foil and fill with weights or dried beans to press crust together. Bake at 425 degrees for 8 minutes. Remove weights and bake 5 more minutes to lightly brown.

Process almond paste, remaining 2/3 cup butter and eggs in mixer until smooth. Pour into crusts. Arrange peaches on top. Bake at 375 for 25 minutes, shielding edges with foil, if necessary, to prevent overbrowning. Remove from oven and cool. Serve with brandy sauce.

Brandy Sauce:
- 1 cup sugar
- 2 teaspoons cornstarch
- 2 cups whipping cream
- 7 egg yolks
- ¼ cup peach brandy

Cook the sugar, cornstarch and cream in a saucepan over medium heat, stirring until sugar dissolves.

Whisk the yolks until frothy, and add some of the warmed cream into the yolks to keep the eggs from scrambling. Pour the yolks into the hot mixture very slowly, while stirring.

Cook over medium heat stirring constantly until thickened. Remove from heat and stir in brandy. Makes 3 cups.

"Women are like tea bags. They don't know how strong they are until they get into hot water." Eleanor Roosevelt

Pink Clouds

Eleanor Roosevelt (1884-1962) has been called "a wallflower that bloomed." During her marriage to President Franklin Roosevelt, her determination and activity to replace his crippled legs, made the world aware of her. She wrote a regular newspaper column for years called "My Day." She also wrote *This Is My Story, This I Remember, On My Own,* and *Tomorrow Is Now.*

One evening in April, 1933, pilot Amelia Earhart (1897-1937) was dining with First Lady Eleanor Roosevelt and others at the White House. Earhart had written two books, *The Fun Of It* and *20 HRS. 40 MIN.* The two became so engrossed in their discussion of flying that Eleanor asked Amelia to take her up in a plane to fly over Washington, D.C. They left the dinner party dressed in long gowns and high heels, took a short flight (after Amelia had her twin-motor airplane readied) and returned.

When they went back to the White House, since the dinner party was over, they had their own special dessert, which Mrs. Roosevelt dubbed "Pink Clouds" in honor of her guest who flew through clouds in her airplane. She asked the chef to put strawberries and whipped cream tinted red on top of angel food cake. They ate it and laughed about their evening.

The admiration for Amelia Earhart caused Eleanor Roosevelt to get a student's pilot license and take flying lessons.

The story of this adventure by these two strong women has caused a children's book to be written called *Eleanor and Amelia Go Flying.*

"Too much of a good thing is wonderful." Mae West (1893-1980)

Prunes

Alice B. Toklas included this recipe for prunes in her cookbook, the same one that included the recipe for hashish brownies. Alice was probably beloved by Gertrude Stein because she was a witty person but an excellent listener who never needed to be the center of attention.

In their Parisian salon, Gertrude advised other writers like Ernest Hemingway about writing until her own shortcomings became apparent. Her soul mate, Alice, may have become more famous as time has passed.

Toklas and Stein had many unusual features about their salon or apartment in Paris. One was that they kept fresh lobsters in water in the bathtub and took them out to cook on various occasions. Toklas joked that the lobsters kept Hemingway from jumping in the tub when he got too drunk.

- 48 pitted prunes
- Port to cover prunes (about 2 cups)
- 1 cup sugar
- 1 pint cream, whipped
- Macaroons

Soak the prunes in enough port to cover for 24 hours. Remove the prunes and add 1 more cup of port and the sugar. Mix well.

Place in a saucepan, add the prunes and bring to a boil. Boil 1 minute. Allow the prunes to cool in the wine.

Refrigerate for 24-36 hours. Serve with whipped cream and garnish with crumbled macaroons.

"When I see a bird that walks like a duck and swims like a duck and quacks like a duck, I call that bird a duck." James Whitcomb Riley

Pudding Cake

James Whitcomb Riley (1849-1916) was known as a Hoosier poet who endeared himself to the whole country before he died. The son of a lawyer-politician, Riley did not excel in school and took up art, sign painting and working medicine shows. He later began to write for newspapers and became a verse humorist. He wrote Rhymes of Childhood, Home Folks, a six volume work of humorous poems. He also created characters such as the Raggedy Man and Little Orphan Annie.

This recipe is from the *James Whitcomb Riley Cookbook*. It was called "Indiana Persimmon Almond Pudding Cake."

- ½ cup butter
- 1 ¼ cups sugar
- 2 eggs
- 1 ¾ cups all-purpose flour
- 1 ½ teaspoons baking powder
- ¼ teaspoon salt
- ½ teaspoon baking soda
- 1 cup sieved persimmon pulp
- ¼ cup buttermilk
- 1 cup ground almonds
- Powdered sugar

Preheat oven to 350 degrees. In a large bowl, beat butter and sugar together until very light. Add eggs one at a time and beat until smooth.

In a small bowl, stir flour with baking powder, salt, and soda. Add dry ingredients alternately with persimmon pulp. Put ripe persimmons through a rice or mash and sieve them. Stir into the butter, eggs mixture, add the buttermilk, and stir in the ground almonds.

Pour into a greased 10" tube pan. Bake for 45-55 minutes or until a toothpick inserted comes out clean.

Cool in the pan about 15 minutes before turning out. If desired, sprinkle each slice with powdered sugar and garnish with fresh red and green grapes.

Makes about 12 servings.

"What calls back the past, like the rich pumpkin pie?"
John Greenleaf Whittier (1807-1892)

Pumpkin Cheesecake

Nancy Bishop, co-author of *Before You Say 'I Quit'* with the editor of this cookbook, has also written a career book and numerous columns on the Texas nightclub scene. She offered this recipe, created by her friend, Julie Fleming, a co-worker who baked pies and cinnamon rolls for Texas businesses.

- 3 8-ounce packages of cream cheese
- ¼ cup brown sugar
- ¾ cup sugar
- 5 eggs
- ¼ cup whipping cream
- 1 can pumpkin
- 1 teaspoon cinnamon

- ½ teaspoon nutmeg
- ¼ teaspoon ground cloves
- Crust of 8-10 cinnamon graham crackers
- 6 tablespoons melted butter
- 1/3 cup pecans
- 1 tablespoon sugar

Use a food processor to grind the crust ingredients (last 4) until crumbly. Press into a spring form pan after spraying with non-stick spray. Whip cream cheese and sugar together until fluffy. Add eggs one at a time, beating after each. Add cream, spices, and pumpkin. Blend. Pour into prepared crust and bake at 350 degrees for 1 hour.

"Cherry ripe, ripe, ripe, I cry,
Full and fair ones; come and buy!"
Robert Herrick (1591-1674)

Rice Pudding

Dinah Shore (1917-1994), popular singer and television personality during the 1940s and 1950s, wrote a cookbook called *Someone's in the Kitchen with Dinah*. She often asked others to contribute recipes to her book.

She claimed that it took her ten years to wheedle this recipe from the Las Vegas Riviera Hotel's owner. This recipe is available on the Internet.

- ½ cup rice (not Minute Rice)
- 1 cup water with 1 teaspoon salt

- 1 quart whole milk
- 4 tablespoons butter
- 3 whole eggs
- ½ cup sugar
- ¾ teaspoon vanilla
- 1 tablespoon cinnamon (optional)
- 3 tablespoons sugar (optional)
- Dried cherries (optional)

Cook the rice according to package directions, but just for half the time. Stir in the milk and butter. Bring up to a boil, reduce heat to very low, cover and cook slowly for about one hour. Stir about every 5 minutes to keep mixture from sticking.

Meanwhile, beat the eggs; add sugar and vanilla. Mix some of the hot milk and the rice into the egg mixture to "temper" it, so it will not curdle. Combine the warmed eggs into the rice pudding pot; cook a few more minutes, stirring until the pudding thickens.

Serve hot or cold with a mixture of sugar and cinnamon. Serves 6.

A delightful option is dried cherries.

"My advice to you is not to inquire why or whither, but just enjoy your ice cream while it's on your plate." Thornton Wilder (1897-1975)

Shortcake

William Wordsworth (1770-1850), English poet, served these short-cakes in his Dove Cottage in Grasmere, Cumbria, England around 200 years ago. The name of the recipe is "English Lakeland Chocolate Caramel Shortcake." This recipe is available on the Internet.

- 1 ½ cups flour
- 1/3 cup sugar
- 6 ounces butter
- 4 ounces butter
- ½ cup sugar
- 1 can condensed milk
- 6 ounces semi-sweet chocolate

To make the base of the shortcake, soften 6 ounces of butter and mix with the flour and 1/3 cup sugar. Spread in a well-buttered 9 x 13 pan. Bake at 350 degrees until golden brown. Cool.

To make the caramel, place 4 ounces of butter, ½ cup sugar and the milk in a saucepan. Stir constantly until the mixture boils. Boil 5 minutes while stirring. Spread over the cake base. Cool.

Melt the chocolate and spread over the caramel. When the chocolate is solid, cut into squares.

"Many people claim coffee inspires them, but, as everybody knows, coffee only makes boring people even more boring." Honore de Balzac (1799-1850)

Tiramisu

Sophia Loren, Italian actress of many movies, has written a cookbook called *Sophia Loren's Recipes and Memories*. She recently described this dessert from her book as the "date food" of the 1980s.

"Tiramisu" is Italian for "pull me up", suggesting that an Italian tired from work, amore, or life can gain a little zip by eating it.

- 3 eggs, separated
- 5 tablespoons sugar
- 6 ounces Mascarpone cheese
- 1 package of about 36 ladyfingers
- 1 cup orange liqueur
- 1 cup espresso coffee
- 2 ounces, grated, bitter chocolate
- ½ cup unsweetened cocoa powder OR
- 2 ounces grated bittersweet chocolate

Combine egg yolks and sugar in bowl and beat well. In a separate bowl, beat egg whites to stiff peaks. In a third bowl, combine egg yolk mixture with the mascarpone, then fold in egg whites to produce a creamy mixture.

Arrange a tight layer of ladyfingers in a 9 X 12 inch serving dish. Using a spoon, drizzle about half the liqueur and half the espresso over the ladyfingers. Cover the ladyfingers with the Mascarpone mixture and the grated chocolate, and dust it with a little more than half the cocoa.

Cover the filling with a second layer of ladyfingers and drizzle with the remaining liqueur and espresso. Place in the refrigerator for 12 hours. Top with the remaining cocoa before serving. Tiramisu can be made 24 hours in advance. Serves 8.

"Seize the moment. Remember all those women on the Titanic who waved off the dessert cart?" Erma Bombeck (1927-1996)

Torte

This torte is based on Sigmund Freud's (1856-1939) favorite recipe. The psychoanalyst developed a tradition of seeing patients on the couch in his home office for approximately an hour. But somewhere along the way, the tradition of seeing patients for only 50 minutes arose.

Legend has it that Freud would prepare this torte, pop it into the oven as his patient rang the doorbell, then remove the torte 50 minutes later as the patient was leaving, thus establishing the 50 minute psychoanalytic session. Seattle psychoanalyst and medical author, Dr. James B. Kludt, contributed it.

- 6 eggs, separated, at room temperature
- ¾ cup white granulated sugar
- 1 tablespoon orange juice concentrate
- 1 tablespoon orange extract
- 1 tablespoon freshly grated orange peel
- 1 cup shelled filberts, roasted, ground

In the bowl of an electric mixer, beat the egg yolks for about three minutes on high; reduce speed to medium and add sugar slowly. Turn speed to high and beat for five minutes. Reduce speed and add concentrate, extract, peel and the filberts (roasted 20 minutes at 350 degrees and coarsely ground).

In a separate bowl, beat the egg whites, adding a pinch of salt, until they are stiff.

Into the egg yolk/orange mixture, gently fold 1/3 of the egg whites, repeat with more, finally adding all the whites. Pour into a buttered 9-inch spring-form pan. Rotate the pan briskly a few times to settle the mixture.

Bake at 325 degrees for 50 minutes or more, inserting a toothpick in the center until it comes out dry. Remove from the oven. Use a knife to ease edges if necessary, release from the pan onto a serving platter. If the torte top is uneven, trim with a sharp knife, or later use the frosting to level the top. Cool.

Bittersweet Torte Frosting:
- 6 tablespoons unsalted butter, room temperature
- ¼ cup granulated sugar
- 1 tablespoon orange extract
- 1 tablespoon orange juice concentrate
- 1 egg
- 3 oz. unsweetened chocolate

In the bowl of an electric mixer, beat the butter at high speed for several minutes; then gradually add the sugar. After all sugar is added, beat at high speed for a few minutes. Then add extract, concentrate and the egg.

In the top of a double boiler, melt the chocolate. Cool slightly, then pour into the frosting batter and mix for several minutes. Apply frosting to the cooled torte with a spatula. Decorate with nuts, cherries or slivered almonds if desired. Serve chilled or at room temperature. Serves 8-10.

"Life's a pudding full of plums;
Care's a canker that benumbs
Wherefore waste our elocution
On impossible solutions?"
Sir William S. Gilbert (1836-1911)

Trifle

Dinah Shore (1917-1994), popular singer and television personality during the 1940s and 1950s, wrote a cookbook called *Someone's in the Kitchen with Dinah*. This Italian pudding dish was one of her favorite recipes.

- 2 cups apricot or plum preserves
- ¼ cup cherry-flavored liqueur
- 1 small box vanilla pudding, prepared
- 1 layer fudge cake, halved
- 15 ounce can cherries, pitted, drained
- 1 cup whipped cream
- ½ cup almonds, toasted

Mix jam with liqueur. Spread jam on cake sides. Put together and cut in 2 inch squares. Put ½ of custard on bottom of bowl.

Top with one half of cake. Press. Top with one half of cherries, more custard, more cake, mash, more cherries.

Top with whipped cream and sprinkle almonds on top.

"God gives the nuts but he does not crack them." Proverb

Tujaque's Pecan Pie

Malcolm Hebert, author of *California Wine Lovers' Cookbook* and other works, whose family owned the famous Tujaque's restaurant in New Orleans for 70 years. The second oldest restaurant in New Orleans, it has been in its current location in the French Quarter since 1856. Hebert described their pecan pie recipe below.

- 1 9-inch unbaked pie shell
- 3 eggs
- 1 cup sugar
- 2/3 cup dark Karo syrup
- 2 tablespoons butter, melted
- 1 teaspoon vanilla extract
- 1/8 teaspoon salt
- 3 tablespoons brandy
- 1 ½ cup pecan halves

"When the French settled in New Orleans, they discovered the pecan. And they promptly made good use of it by creating pecan brittle, pecan pralines, pecan sauce and of course pecan pie. The first pecans I ever ate came from my Grandmother's pecan tree in her backyard. Every Christmas she would send a 50-pound gunny sack of pecans to my mother. My Grandmother's pecans were not those tasteless thin-shelled kind; hers had thick shells with just as much shell as meat and ten times more taste.

"Preheat the oven to 400 degrees. In a glass mixing bowl, beat the eggs, blending in the sugar, syrup, butter, vanilla, salt, brandy and pecans. Pour the mixture into the pie shell and bake 10 minutes. Lower the oven to 350 degrees and bake 30 minutes or until a wooden skewer or knife inserted into the pie comes out clean. Cool on a wire rack. Serves 6 to 8."

"When one has tasted watermelon he knows what the angels eat." Mark Twain (1835-1910)

Water and Honey Melons

The world's oldest cookbook was written by Apicius (1st century) who taught haute cuisine to the chefs in the court of the Roman emperors. This interesting hot dish combined melons with unusual tastes.

- ½ honey melon
- ½ watermelon
- Passum (honey)
- 1 tablespoon parsley, minced
- ½ teaspoon fresh ground black pepper
- Salt to taste

Peel, seed and dice the melons. Combine all and cook until done. Salt according to taste.

"I am a writer who came of a sheltered life. A sheltered life can be a daring life as well. For all serious daring starts from within." Eudora Welty (1909-2001)

White Fruit Cake

Eudora Welty (1909-2001) attended Mississippi State College for Women and despite a "sheltered life", made a photographic collection of Mississippi life for the W.P.A. She wrote short stories and novels, among which were *The Optimist's Daughter, Why I Live at the P.O., A Curtain of Green, The Ponder Heart* and *One Writer's Beginnings.*

She got this recipe from her friend, Mrs. J. A. Mosal. She wrote, "I often think to make a friend's fine recipe is to celebrate her once more, and in that cheeriest, most aromatic of places to celebrate in—the home kitchen."

- 1 ½ cups butter
- 2 cups sugar
- 6 eggs
- 1 teaspoon grated nutmeg
- 1 teaspoon vanilla
- 1 cup whiskey plus more for soaking
- 4 cups sifted flour
- 2 teaspoons baking powder
- 1 pound chopped pecans
- 1 pound crystallized cherries, red + green
- 1 pound crystallized pineapple

Cut fruit in small pieces and dust with 1 cup flour. Cream butter and sugar well. Add eggs one at a time. Sift dry ingredients with remaining 3 cups of flour. Add this to sugar mixture alternating with whiskey.

When well blended, add fruit and pecans. Bake in a tube pan at 225 degrees for about 2 hours.

When done, pour ¼ to ½ cup whiskey over while still hot. Serves 20-24.

Chapter 10

COOKIES AND CANDY

Animal Crackers

Animal crackers, and cocoa to drink,
That is the finest of suppers, I think;
When I'm grown up and can have what I please,
I think I shall always insist upon these.
Christopher Morley (1890-1957)

"'Oh, Fudge!' is frequently uttered to reflect dismay or disappointment. It comes from the word 'futsch', meaning 'gone, ruined.' A German candy maker, while making chocolate caramels, made a serious ingredient error and instead of a smooth textured batch, it had a slight 'grain.' Rather than dispose of it, he cut it into squares and named it 'futsch' and sold it as his newly discovered creation." Virginia Holen

Almond Fudge

This is Virginia Holen's family recipe from her book *Hazel's Candies Copper Kettle Trade Secrets*. Virginia grew up on a farm in Washington State, next to the oldest of six children.

She attended Central Washington University. After World War II, the family opened a candy shop. They became the largest candy manufacturer in Washington.

- 3 ounces whipping cream
- 1 ½ cups granulated sugar
- ¼ cup lite Karo Corn syrup
- 2 tablespoons butter
- ½ teaspoon salt
- ¼ cup plus 1 tablespoon Marshmallow crème
- 1 ounce coarsely chopped blanched almonds
- 1-2 ounces red and/or green candied cherries
- 1 ½ teaspoon pure almond extract
- Read recipe for equipment before starting

Grease 1 ½ quart kettle sides with butter. On medium, bring whipping cream to a boil. Set off heat. Add sugar and stir to melt. Stir in Karo, butter and salt.

With thermometer in kettle, bring batch to a boil and cook to 220 degrees, stirring just enough to keep from sticking to the kettle bottom. With a pastry brush dipped in cold water, wash around and above the cook line. Repeat a second time. Continue to stir and cook to 238 degrees. Note: Watch the thermometer after the wash down and it will reach 238 degrees quickly. Remove from burner and set on a wire rack to cool for 5 minutes.

With rubber spatula or large serving spoon, stir in remaining ingredients. Continue to stir 5-10 minutes, working kettle sides and bottom. Gloss will begun to dull and fudge will have a thickening appearance, as if trying to hold a shape. Without delay, scoop into a loaf pan for a thickness of about 1 ¼". As soon as the batch sets, remove from the pan and place on wire cooling rack. When cold, store in plastic bag to mellow overnight for better cutting.

"Tell me what you eat, and I will tell you what you are." Anthelme Brillat-Savarin (1755-1826)

Alice B. Toklas' Brownies

The Autobiography of Alice B. Toklas (1877-1967) was written in 1933 by Gertrude Stein. Toklas was Stein's lover and publisher. The two lived in France and traveled together in Europe during the 1920s and 1930s and Stein died in 1946.

In 1954, Toklas compiled the *Alice B. Toklas Cookbook* and included a recipe by painter Brion Gysin for "Hashish Fudge."

At first, publishers refused to print it but they soon relented and made Alice much more famous in Bohemian circles than she already was. "Cannibus sativa" is marijuana.

"Take 1 teaspoon of black peppercorns, 1 whole nutmeg, 4 sticks of cinnamon, 1 teaspoon coriander, and pulverize them in a mortar. Then take 1 handful dates, 1 handful dried figs, 1 handful shelled almonds, and 1 handful peanuts. Chop and mix together.

"A bunch of cannibus sativa can be pulverized. This and the spices should be dusted over the mixed fruit and nuts, and kneaded together. Add about 1 cup sugar dissolved in a big pat of butter. Roll into a cake and cut into pieces or make into balls the size of walnuts.

"It should be eaten with care. Two pieces are quite sufficient. Obtaining the cannibus may present certain difficulties… It should be picked and dried as soon as it has gone to seed and while the plant is still green."

"Never eat more than you can lift." Miss Piggy

Christmas Sugar Cookies

Dolly Parton, entertainer, song writer and author, is also very funny. She said, "It costs a lot to make a person look this cheap," referring to her blonde hairdo, glossy fingernails, overly made up glittering persona.

She wrote songs such as *9 to 5, Here You Come Again, Jolene, Coat of Many Colors, I Will Always Love You, My Tennessee Mountain Home, Down from Dover,* and many more. She has written several books including *Grand Ole Opry History of Country Music, Just the Way I Am, Coat of Many Colors, Dolly Parton: I Will Always Love You,* and *Dolly: My Life and Other Unfinished Business.*

- 1 cup sugar
- 3 cups sifted flour
- 1 ½ teaspoon grated lemon rind

- 2 cups butter, softened
- 2 large egg yolks

Cream sugar and butter in a bowl. Beat in eggs, then flour and lemon peel. Knead gently together. Don't overwork the dough, but make sure it's consistent. Chill dough for 3 hours. Preheat oven to 350 degrees. Roll out dough with a rolling pin. Cut into shapes and place on greased cookie sheets. Bake until tops are pinkish-brown, about 8 minutes. Makes 12 to 24 cookies, depending on size.

"When men reach their sixties and retire, they go to pieces. Women just go right on cooking." Gail Sheehy

Coconut Candy

Greta Manville, co-author of *The Purgatory Trail*, got this recipe from her grandfather who lived in Miami where coconuts were readily available.

Greta has written four novels since 1992, three of which were suspense mysteries. She has won several fiction and poetry contests. *The Purgatory Trail* is the story of several female writers who traveled with a cowboy to learn his way of life. The web site is www.purgatorytrail.com.

- 3 cups sugar
- Water enough to saturate sugar
- 1 coconut, peeled, grated or ground

Cook the sugar and water, stirring constantly, until the mixture spins a thread when tested in a cup of water. (A candy thermometer should show 230-240 degrees.) Add coconut and continue to cook and stir until water in the mixture disappears from the sides of the pan and the mixture makes a rustling sound. Pour into butter pans to cool.

"My wife is on a constant diet. Coconuts and bananas. She hasn't lost any weight but she sure can climb a tree!" Henny Youngman (1906-1998)

Coconut Cookies

Dinah Shore (1917-1994), singer and television personality during the 1940s and 1950s, also wrote a cookbook called *Someone's in the Kitchen with Dinah.* The surprises about this recipe are the pecans and the corn syrup glaze on the cookies.

- 2 cups flour, sifted
- ½ teaspoon baking soda
- 1 cup butter or margarine
- ½ teaspoon vanilla extract
- 1 cup sugar
- 1 egg, well beaten
- 3 ½ cups shredded moist coconut
- 1 egg yolk
- 1 tablespoon cream
- 1 ½ cups pecan halves
- ½ cup white corn syrup

Stir together flour and baking soda; set aside. Cream butter until softened. Gradually add vanilla, creaming until fluffy. Add sugar in thirds, beating thoroughly after each addition.

Blend egg and 2 cups coconut in a bowl; mix thoroughly. Stir in dry ingredients. Knead lightly with fingertips 5-10 times or until the mixture holds together. Spread the remaining coconut onto waxed paper. Form dough into 6 rolls (about 1 inch in diameter) and roll in coconut.

Wrap in waxed paper and place in refrigerator at least 3 hours. Preheat oven to 325 degrees. Meanwhile, lightly grease a cookie sheet. Remove rolls from the refrigerator and, with a sharp knife, cut crosswise in ½ inch slices. Place on the cookie sheet ¾ inch apart.

Mix egg yolk and cream together and brush cookie tops. Press pecan halves on top of each cookie. Bake about 20 minutes or until lightly browned. Remove to cooling rack. Heat corn syrup until warm. Glaze cookies by brushing tops. Makes 8 dozen.

"Avoid fruits and nuts. You are what you eat." Jim Davis (Garfield)

Date Nut Candy

Greta Manville, co-author of *The Purgatory Trail*, wrote humorously about modern women who went on an adventure to learn about cowboy life. It is unlikely that they had the amenities to fix this recipe during their journeys.

Greta earned a B.A. and M.A. in English at San Jose State University. A former transportation careerist, she writes and is working on a bibliography for the works of John Steinbeck on a fellowship at San Jose State University. She considered creating some recipes spoofing his works such as "Cannery Row Beans" and "Flat Tortillas." This is her own recipe and a very good one.

- 2 ½ cups sugar
- 2/3 cup milk
- 1 cup chopped dates
- 1 cup chopped nuts
- 1 tablespoon butter

Boil sugar and milk until mixture forms a soft ball in water (234 degrees.) Add dates. Boil to form a ball (238 degrees.) Add nuts and butter. Cool slightly. Beat until mixture becomes stiff. Pour over wet towel and roll to shape a log. Cool before cutting into slices.

"In after-dinner talk, across the walnuts and the wine." Alfred, Lord Tennyson (1809-1892)

Fudge (Always Perfect)

Jean Homme, short story writer, retired to Sun City, Arizona, from Minneapolis, Minnesota.

- 2 cups sugar
- ½ cup milk
- 2 squares unsweetened Baker's chocolate
- ½ teaspoon salt
- 1 cup butter
- ½ teaspoon vanilla
- 1 cup walnuts

Rent the movie *Chocolat* to get into the right mood for this recipe. Leave the movie long enough to combine sugar, milk, chocolate, salt and butter in a saucepan. Stir only enough to blend. Bring to a boil and boil 2 minutes. Remove from the stove. Place the saucepan in a shallow pan of cold water. Beat it until it thickens. Add vanilla and walnuts and stir them in. Pour into a pan or pie plate and cool in the refrigerator for several hours until set, during which time you can go back and see some more of the movie.

Cut into square pieces and eat it while the credits are running at the end of the movie. This can be made for frosting. Just cut the movie, I mean the recipe in half and boil for only 1 minute.

"There are two kinds of people in the world. Those who love chocolate and communists." Leslie Moak Murray in *"Murray's Law."*

Kahlua Truffles

Virginia Holen wrote *Hazel's Candies Copper Kettle Trade Secrets.* She described how the Truffle nomenclature came from a European genus of fleshy, edible fungi that grew underground and was considered a rare delicacy among epicureans.

Originally, the candy was formed to resemble the fungi, but now it is most frequently round or oblong-shaped for dipping in chocolate or sifted cocoa.

- 12 ounces slivered dipping chocolate
- 2 tablespoons Kahlua liqueur
- ½ cup whipping cream

- ½ cup half and half cream
- 1 cup plus 2 tablespoons white sugar

Foil line a 5 x 9 inch loaf pan, extending foil up and over the long sides. Butter lightly. With a chef's knife, shave the chocolate, then add water to the lower part of a double boiler, keeping it one inch below the top pan.

Heat water to 140 degrees. To the top kettle, add about ¼ of the shaved chocolate, melting after each addition. When well blended and reaches 120 degrees, remove top kettle and cool down to 90 degrees (or feels cool to the inside wrist), then stir in Kahlua. To keep the chocolate fluid, place kettle back over the warm (not hot) water.

In the saucepan, bring the two creams to a boil. Remove from heat. Add sugar, stirring to melt. Bring to a boil on medium heat, then with a pastry brush dipped in cold water, wash around above the foam line. Stirring gently, cook to 220 degrees. Watch closely as it tends to foam. Cool to 100 degrees.

Now, stir the chocolate into the 'just warm' cream. Using the wire whisk, beat the mix until it starts to thicken (about 10 minutes). It will feel a bit cool to the inside wrist. Pour into a prepared pan and refrigerate overnight.

Dipping day: Sift about ¼ cup cocoa onto a wax sheet. Using the large end of a melon-ball cutter, scoop out (or pinch off) marble size pieces, rolling them around in the palms of the hand, then toss into cocoa powder for dusting. Flatten each ball a bit, by pressing gently on top. Cover with wax paper and refrigerate for 30 minutes to firm them up. If you prefer not to chocolate-dip the truffles, they are very tasty when served right from the refrigerator with just the cocoa dusting. If they are to be chocolate coated, allow them to come to room temperature. If the center is too cold, the coating will lose gloss and occasionally crack from internal expansion.

"Venice is like eating an entire box of chocolate liqueurs in one go." Truman Capote (1924-1984)

Miracle Worker Chip Cookies

Erma Bombeck (1927-1996) wrote this comical recipe story in *Forever, Erma*. The recipe is unfinished so we leave you to your own comical devices to try it.

"One afternoon last week after a dismal attempt at a banana nut loaf (using no bananas and no nuts), I decided to whip up chocolate chip cookies. The chocolate chip bits were only a two-mile bicycle ride away. I huffed and pedaled until my varicose veins begged for mercy. It took me two hours and ten minutes, round trip.

"Back in the kitchen, I was ready to create when I discovered I was out of flour and brown sugar. I'll share with you my recipe for the Miracle Worker Chip Cookies. Substitute a cup of oatmeal for the flour and add a teaspoonful of vanilla. If you don't have the vanilla, use lemon extract with a dash...."

"Candy is dandy but liquor is quicker."
Reflections on "Ice-Breaking"
Ogden Nash (1902-1971)

Peanut Brittle

Virginia Holen wrote *Hazel's Candies Copper Kettle Trade Secrets* using family recipes over 100 years old. This recipe is called "Old Fashioned Peanut Brittle." At an Oregon demonstration, someone forgot to add corn syrup and before a huge crowd, the peanut brittle didn't flow but just came out in one big blob, which quickly turned to sugar. Virginia could only say, "Old candymakers never die, they just grain away!"

When Virginia met her husband, he bet her $10 that she wouldn't marry him. When she did marry him, he would not pay off because he wanted to see if it would last. They just celebrated their 60th wedding anniversary.

- ¾ cup water
- 2 ¼ cups granulated sugar
- ¾ cup Karo lite corn syrup
- 1 ½ teaspoons salt
- 1 ½ cup raw Spanish peanuts
- 1 tablespoon butter
- 1 ½ teaspoon pure vanilla
- 1 ½ teaspoon baking soda
- Read recipe for utensils before starting

Bring water to boil in a 3 quart kettle with a lid. Turn off heat, add sugar, and stir to melt. Stir in corn syrup and salt. Bring to boil, place lid on kettle, and allow to steam for 3 minutes. Remove lid and put in thermometer. Do not stir until thermometer reaches 220 degrees then use a pastry brush dipped in cold water to remove sugar granules above cook line. Heat to 240 and add peanuts, stirring constantly until reaching 270 degrees.

Add butter in a wooden stir stick and let melt. At 285-290 degrees, remove from heat. Let cool for a minute or so then add vanilla. Stir, then add baking soda and stir briskly then pour quickly on an oiled, flour-dusted warm marble slab or backside of an 18" x 24" Baker's bun pan. Use a spatula to spread the brittle and evenly distribute the peanuts.

With flour-dusted gloves, stretch the outside edges then work toward the thick center area. As it cools, use a Chef's knife sawing to cut the batch in half, flip over and continue to stretch all areas. While still warm, flip a second time to keep the peanuts and syrup balanced.

To avoid moisture, place in a plastic bag as soon as the heat has dissipated.

"Legend had it that a candy maker living at the seashore left a pan of unpulled taffy in his screened-in porch overnight. A storm came up and the candy was sprayed with a mist of salt water. In the morning, after a taste, he knew this confection was unique. He named it Saltwater Taffy." Virginia Holen

Salt Water Taffy

Virginia Holen, author of *Hazel's Candies Copper Kettle Trade Secrets,* divulged this one-of-a-kind candy recipe for the novice. Her book even describes how to "stripe the batch" plus including variations on this and other basic candy recipes, and can be purchased on www.amazon.com. After she retired, she spent eight years testing batches of candies, reducing formulas in size, to write the definitive book on candy.

- ½ cup water
- 1 cup granulated sugar
- ¾ cup lite Karo corn syrup
- Lecithin (dab on the tip of a knife)
- 1 ½ teaspoons salt
- ¼ cup hard butter (1 ounce corn oil containing lecithin can be substituted)
- Flavoring if desired

Bring water to a boil. Set off the heat and add sugar, stirring to melt. Then add corn syrup, lecithin and salt. Stir well, bring to a boil and steam with a lid for 3 minutes. Remove the lid and add the thermometer.

Boil a few minutes, then with a pastry brush dipped in cold water, wash around and above the cook line to remove any sugar crystals. Repeat at 230 degrees. Then add hard butter, stirring only enough to mix.

Without further stirring, cook to 252 degrees, and pour immediately on lightly oiled marble slab or bun pan but do not scrape the cook kettle. As the outer edges begin to cool, with a spatula, gently fold them into the warmer area. When cool enough to handle, begin to pull with buttered fingertips. As the batch begins to firm up, add flavoring to taste and continue to pull about 14 minutes or until the batch takes on a dry, satiny stage.

When the proper consistency is reached, pull a strip about 1 inch wide and 3/8" thick, smoothing it with the side of your palm, then cut into 5 inch strips. Continue to work from the main bulk with short, drawing motions, stripping and smoothing between thumb and index finger.

As pieces are cut, your helper will shape and smooth the strip before placing it in the center of a 6" x 6" dry-wax paper square, rolling it over to the other flat side, making a snug fold. Have an 8" x 8" cake pan nearby to stack strips to cool. If the batch is not pulled long enough, the sticks tend to lead at the ends.

"The Carpenter said nothing but 'The butter's spread too thick!'" Lewis Carroll (1832-1898)

Sherlock's Thumbprint Cookies

An enterprising cook came up with a literary title for cookies that have a thumbprint. There is also a *Sherlock Holmes Cookbook* with dishes appropriate to London where the fictional detective, created by Sir Arthur Conan Doyle (1859-1930), was said to have lived.

Doyle's father was a civil servant who supplemented wages with book illustrations and sketches at criminal trials. He became mentally ill and was hospitalized, leaving his mother to run a boarding house to make ends meet. Doyle became a physician who specialized in eyes and practiced from 1885-1891.

He retired to write full time and his Sherlock Holmes, with exceedingly astute "eyes," was often pictured with a magnifying glass to see even better. Holmes also used cocaine in early novels, an anesthetic used in eye surgery and other procedures. It is unknown whether Doyle used cocaine. Doyle ran for Parliament but lost and after the death of his first invalid wife, he remarried.

He was knighted before WWI. He grew tired of the Sherlock Holmes character and killed him off, but when subscriptions to the magazine featuring Holmes dropped dramatically, he re-instituted the character in *The Hound of the Baskervilles.*

- ½ cup sugar
- 1 cup butter, softened
- 1 teaspoon vanilla
- 2 egg yolks
- 2 ¼ cups all purpose flour
- 1 teaspoon baking powder
- ¼ cup jam or any flavor of preserves

Make a spot of tea, Sherlock's favorite beverage, to sip on whilst you compose these cookies.

In a medium bowl, beat the sugar, butter, vanilla and egg yolks until light and fluffy. Gradually add flour and baking powder, mix well. Cover with plastic wrap and refrigerate 30 minutes. Heat the oven to 350 degrees. Shape the dough into one inch balls. Place 2 inches apart on a baking sheet.

With your thumb, make an imprint in the center of each cookie. Allow the swirls on your finger tip to show so that even Dr. Watson can detect just who made the cookies. Bake them 11 to 14 minutes. Spoon ½ teaspoon jam into the center of each cookie. Cool completely.

Be careful when eating not to drop any crumbs on your clothes or Sherlock will have his magnifying glass out to detect just what you've eaten, when and where you were when the hound of the Baskervilles was howling.

"Everything I like is either illegal, immoral or fattening." Alexander Woolcott (1887-1943)

Sinful Christmas Cookies

Sinclair Lewis (1885-1951) wrote *Main Street, Babbitt, It Can Happen Here, Arrowsmith, Elmer Gantry, Cass Timberlane,* and other books.

John Koblas' book *Sinclair Lewis: Home at Last,* describes this recipe as Lewis' favorite one for Christmas cookies. This recipe is available on the Internet.

- ½ pound butter
- ½ cup finely chopped almonds
- 2 eggs
- 1 shot glass bourbon
- 2 cups sugar
- 2 tablespoons Droste's cocoa
- 2 cups flour

Make sure you mix the ingredients well. Otherwise several of the cookies will have a very strong taste. Refrigerate mixture overnight. Drop little balls on a well-greased cookie sheet for 8-10 minutes in a 375 degree oven. If you can smell them cooking, they are done.

Chapter 11

THIS AND THAT

Writer's Block Recipe

The first recorded incident of writer's block occurred in 1355. A man named Herbert Woodson was sitting down to write a novel about pantaloon when, all of a sudden, his mind went blank. Thinking his brain had sprung a leak, he immediately encased his head in Lucite. The next morning, the maid found his body and the block of Lucite on the floor. Thinking he was asleep, she just vacuumed around him. The next day, the milkman came and found the corpse lying on the floor with the Lucite on its head. He alerted all the townspeople and they called his condition "writer's block" (mostly because he was a writer with a block of Lucite on his head.)

They then banned all Lucite from the tri-county area. Naturally, they were right in doing so because it was the Lucite that killed Herbert Woodson. Lucite, you see, is a syrupy liquid that hardens quickly. The chemist, Lucas Williams, invented it in 1301. He was busy making pancakes one day when he found that he was out of maple syrup. He began pouring chemicals carelessly into a vat, hoping to create a suitable topping for his breakfast. He scooped some up in a bowl and was about to pour the mixture onto his pancakes when he noticed it had hardened and was stuck to the inside of the bowl. He realized he had created quite a substance. So he did what any respected chemist would do. He bottled it and sold it as a sports drink and called it Lucarade.

Writer's block can strike anyone at any time. The only way to prevent it is to drink a glass of Lucarade. If you can't find that, fill a straight-sided glass with 1/3 cheap vodka and 2/3 tap water. Drink slowly, at home, as you write. Repeat until your great American novel is finished or you are 40, whichever comes first. Joseph Cabrera

"When choosing between two evils, I always like to take the one I've never tried before." Mae West (1893-1980)

Arsenic Entree

Dashiell Hammett (1894-1961) wrote the Thin Man mysteries and many other novels and short stories. In "Fly Paper", originally written in 1924, he described how a person might ingest arsenic gradually so that they could join a victim in eating an entrée with arsenic and yet survive.

"Suppose you were to take a milligramme of this poison the first day, two miligrammes the second day, and so on. Well, at the end of ten days you would have taken a centigramme: at the end of twenty days increasing another milligramme, you would have taken three hundred centigrammes; that is to say, a dose you would support without inconvenience, and which would be very dangerous for any other person who had not taken the same precautions as yourself... Her body accustomed to it, taking steadily increasing doses, so when she slipped the big shot in Babe's food she could eat it with him without danger."

"Oats in Scotland are food for Scotchmen; but in England food for horses," said Dr. Samuel Johnson (1709-1784) with disdain.
A Scotchman replied, *"Yes, and where can you find such men as in Scotland, or such horses as in England?"*

Atholl Brose

Writers first recorded this brew in 1475 when the Earl of Atholl was attempting to squelch a rebellion against the King of Scotland. Hearing that the rebel, Iain MacDonald, drank from a small well, the Earl ordered it to be filled with honey, whisky and oatmeal. MacDonald lingered too long sampling the brew and was captured! The Duke of Atholl made the recipe public some years ago.

- 3 rounded tablespoons of medium oatmeal
- 2 tablespoons of heather honey
- Scotch whisky

Put the oatmeal in a basin and mix it with cold water until the consistency is that of a thick paste. Leave it for half an hour and then put it through a fine strainer, pressing with a wooden spoon to extract as much liquid as possible. Throw away the oatmeal and use the creamy liquor from the oatmeal for the brose.

Mix four teaspoonfuls of the honey and 4 tablespoons of the prepared oatmeal and stir well. Put into a quart bottle and fill with malt whisky. Shake before serving.

"When we lose, I eat. When we win, I eat. I also eat when we're rained out."
Tommy Lasorda

Barbecue Sauce

Cajun entertainer and chef Justin Wilson (1886-1975) wrote *Outside Cooking With Inside Help*. His barbecue sauce recipe from that cookbook is one of his best and is available on the Internet.

- 3 cups onions, chopped
- ¼ cup honey

- 1 tablespoon garlic, chopped
- 2 tablespoons lemon juice
- 1 cup sweet pepper, chopped
- 1 tablespoon salt
- ½ cup parsley, dried
- 3 tablespoons Lea & Perrins
- 1 cup dry white wine
- ½ teaspoon mint, dried
- 3 tablespoons vinegar
- 1 tablespoon Liquid smoke
- 2 cups ketchup
- ½ tablespoon Louisiana hot sauce

Place all ingredients in a pot that is big enough to hold them. Bring to a boil. Cook, covered, on low heat for several hours. "Dis is a mighty fine sauce, I garontee!"

"I would give you spiced wine to drink, the juice of my pomegranates." Song of Solomon 8:2

Bible Foods

The Bible describes food and drink for nourishment as well as medicinal properties. These quotations display some of the cuisine and culture of those who wrote many books of the Bible.

"Then Isiah said, 'Prepare a poultice of figs." They did so and applied it to the boil, and he recovered." 2 Kings 20:7

"But a Samaritan, as he traveled, came to where the man was; and when he saw him, he took pity on him. He went to him and bandaged his wounds, pouring on oil and wine." Luke 10:33;34

"Then their father Israel said to them: 'If it must be so, then do this: take some of the choice fruits of the land in your bags, and carry down to the man a present, a little balm and a little honey, gum, myrrh, pistachio nuts, and almonds.'" Genesis 43:11

"Then Abigail made haste, and took 200 loaves and two skins of wine and five sheep ready dressed, and five measures of parches grain, and a hundred clusters of raisins, and 200 cakes of figs and laid them on asses." 1 Samuel 25:18.

"No longer drink only water, but use a little wine for the sake of your stomach and your frequent ailments." 1 Timothy 5:23

"Be not among winebibbers, or among gluttonous eaters of meat; for the drunkard and the glutton will come to poverty, and drowsiness will clothe a man with rags." Proverbs 23:20,21.

"Start every day with a smile and get it over with." W. C. Fields (1879-1946)

Black Pepper Experience

Erma Bombeck (1927-1996) wrote about the "Black Pepper Experience" in *Family: The Ties That Bind… and Gag.* After going to a restaurant where every person introduced themselves to the Bombeck family, Erma described what happened.

"When the entrees were placed before us, no one dared touch his food until he had gone through the Black Pepper Experience. Now, I don't pretend to understand when pepper got to be right up there behind frankincense and myrrh, but it is. That's when Stud came over to the table with a pepper mill the size of a piano leg (the bigger the pepper mill…the larger the check) and said, 'Pepper?'

"All the conversation came to a halt while we thought about what our answers would be when it came to us. I hesitated a moment and then said, 'Yes, please.' Stud watched my hand, waiting for me to orchestrate how much and the precise moment to stop.

"The weird part of this is that not one grain of pepper comes out of the mill. (It's sorta like watching the first piece of luggage come off a carousel in airport luggage. Ever see anyone claim it? Of course you haven't. Because it doesn't belong to anyone, that's why.)"

"Many men are like unto sausages: whatever you stuff them with, that they will bear in them." Alexei Tolstoy (1828-1910)

Boudin Blanc

Lewis and Clark had a Frenchman named Charbonneau on their expedition to discover America west of the Mississippi River, accompanied by his Indian wife Sacagawea.

They described a sausage, similar to current Cajun boudin, made by Charbonneau, as well as some other interesting cuisine. They were good observers but lacked some skills in spelling their native language.

Lewis's journal recorded how he selected a fat buffalo and saved "the necessary material for making what our wrighthand cook Charbono calls the *boudin blanc;* this white pudding we all esteem one of the greatest delicacies of the forrest." Lewis described how Charbonneau made the sausage and ended, "It is then baptized in the missouri with two dips and a flirt, and bobbed into the kettle; from when after it be well boiled it is taken and fryed with bears oil until it becomes brown, when it is ready to esswage the pangs of a keen appetite or such as travelers in the wilderness are seldom at a loss for."

Sometimes the expedition had to survive on unusual food. Lewis wrote, "My fare is really sumptuous this evening; buffaloe's humps, tongues and marrowbones, fine trout parched meal pepper and salt." Other times they ate dogs. Lewis recorded, "Fortunately the men were extremely fond of the dog meat; for my own part, I have become so perfectly reconciled to the dog that I think it an agreeable food and would prefer it vastly to lean Venison or Elk."

While meat made up most of their diet, occasionally berries, seeds, nuts and plants were eaten. One of the men found some black morel mushrooms, which Lewis "roasted and eat without salt pepper or grease in this way I had for the first time the true taist of the morel which is truly an insipid taistless food." This is convincing evidence that the highly prized morel mushroom rises above being an insipid tasteless food primarily because of the way it is usually prepared and seasoned.

"Fill high the bowl with Samian (from Samos) wine." George Gordon, Lord Byron (1788-1824)

Candide's Meals

Voltaire (1694-1778) wrote a social satire called *Candide*. The adventures of Candide in Italy, Portugal, South America and Turkey with the ever optimistic Dr. Pangloss make for a wonderful satire on the vices of men, as pertinent today as 250 years ago. After adventures and meals like the following, Candide decided, "T'is well but we must cultivate our gardens."

In Peru, they were "served four soups, each garnished with two parrots, a boiled condor which weighed 200 pounds, two roast monkeys of excellent flavor, 300 colibris in one dish and 600 humming birds in another, exquisite ragouts and delicious pastries, all in dishes of a sort of rock-crystal. The boys and girls brought several sorts of drinks made of sugarcane."

In Venice, at the Piazza San Marco, Candide ate "macaroni, Lombardy partridges, caviar, and drank Montepulciano, Lacryma Christi, Cyprus and Samos wine."

In Istanbul, they ate "several kinds of sherbet which they made themselves, caymac flavored with candied citron peel, oranges, lemons, limes, pineapples, dates, pistachios and Mocha coffee which had not been mixed with the bad coffee."

"The French are sawed-off sissies who eat snails and slugs and cheese that smells like people's feet. Utter cowards who force their own children to drink wine, they gibber like baboons even when you try to speak to them in their own wimpy language." P. J. O'Rourke

Caveman Cuisine

In Jean Auel's *The Clan of the Cave Bear,* Iza and Grod prepared a meal using the constant fire that was maintained by an elder. Using wooden bowls filled with water, they added hot stones to boil water and cook vegetables. They skewered and roasted meat. Auel beautifully illustrated the close association between food and medicine in prehistoric life.

"Fat grubs were toasted crisp and small lizards roasted whole until their tough skins blackened and cracked, exposing tasty bits of well-cooked flesh...In another bowl she crushed clover leaves, measured out a quantity of powdered hops into her hand, tore the alder bark into shreds, and poured boiling water over it. Then she ground hard dry meat from their preserved emergency ration into a coarse meal between two stones and mixed the concentrated protein with water from cooking vegetables in a third bowl."

The injured girl expected to eat from the bowls placed near her. She learned that the bowl with clover, hops and bark was a medicinal poultice which they placed on her leg. But she drank the protein vegetable broth.

"All I ask of food is that it doesn't harm me." Michael Palin

Chili Shiska-Bob

Bob Cheney taught history in public schools and college in Dallas for 38 years. He wrote *Interrupted Lives: Hood's Texas Brigade, Tragedy in Black and White, Brushes With Greatness*, and co-authored *American History in Song* and *Dallas and the Jack Ruby Trial*. He also teaches in Elderhostels and local colleges. After proofreading his wife's cookbooks until he was sick to his stomach, he decided to create his own recipe.

Fill a sprayed #2 washtub with water to within 1/3 inch of top. Add ¼ teaspoon chili powder. Fold in 1 cup oatmeal. Blend 1 gallon walnuts with 1 eggplant, unskinned, and refrigerate for 2 months. Combine 2 chopped mushrooms, 1 can sauerkraut, ½ cup tofu and ¼ tablespoon Sanka. Taste before proceeding and adjust seasonings. Next add to tub in this order:

browned lemon zest, 1 Snickers bar, ½ bale hay, 1 pound sliced collard greens and a pinch of red cabbage. Then sauté 2 sliced carrots, puree 1 strand barb wire and mix together with 3 Jonathan apples. Combine all and add 1 pound corkscrew pasta or elbow macaroni. Boil down to evaporate all liquid, package powder in a tightly closed container and send to someone who has not invited you to their parties. Instruct them about blending the powder with a paste of 1 cup pesto, ¼ teaspoon cinnamon, ½ cup olive oil and any deboned, skinned roadkill of their choice, trimmed of fat. Makes 47 ½ servings with additional trips to Dairy Queen or the emergency room.

"I used to be Snow White, but I drifted." Mae West (1893-1980)

Circe's Potion

In Homer's Odyssey, several centuries before the Greek Socratic era, this epic quest took Odysseus through alien territory. When he arrived at the island of the temptress Circe, she tried to make the sailors stay. Homer described how she tried to seduce them with her voice and her potions.

Pramnian wine is a strong wine grown near the Pramnian mountain, and is said to contract the bowels. After Circe turned the men into lustful pigs who wanted only to sleep and have sex, ("male chauvinist pigs") Odysseus had to work very hard to get them back into shape to return to the boat and sail on. To this day, wines made with barley, honey, water and sometimes cheese products are still produced in Greece and Turkey.

"She brought them inside and seated them on chairs and benches, and mixed them a potion, with barley and cheese and pale honey added to Pramneian wine, but put into the mixture malignant drugs, to make them forgetful of their own country. When she had given them this and they had drunk it down, they turned into pigs."

"I don't mind eels except as meals." Ogden Nash (1902-1971)

Coronation Feast for King Henry V

A Noble Book of Royal Feasts compiled by Richard Pynson in 1500 was recently discovered in London and appears to be the first known cookbook printed in English. But that English is hard to read. At the coronation of Henry V in 1413, he was served swans, roasted and probably redressed in their feathers. Everybody else would have eaten conger eel. Trout, fried roach, perch, carp and lamprey eel followed the swan course.

A feast for the Archbishop of York in 1465 included birds such as curlew, gannets, gulls, dotterels, larks, redshanks, peacocks, partridges, woodcocks, knots and chopped sparrows. Such dishes were served with a dash of cinnamon, ginger, saffron or cloves. Colored eggs called "ledlardes" were often used. An example of the recipes is the following direction for making ledlardes.

"To make ledlards of thre colours, take clene cowe mylke and put it in thre pots, and breke to every pot a quantite of egges as ye seme best, and colour one parte with sanders and another parte with saffron and the thyrde parte grene with herbes."

Translation: To make eggs of three colors, take clean cow milk and put it in three pots and break in every pot a quantity of eggs as seems best, and color one part with sanders (yellow from the Sandarac tree) and another part with saffron (red) and the third part green with herbs.

"My illness is due to my doctor's insistence that I drink milk, a whitish fluid they force down helpless babies." W. C. Fields (1879-1946)

Cure for Warts

Mark Twain (Samuel Clemens 1835-1910) wrote a charming discussion between Tom and Huck Finn on how to cure warts in *The Adventures of Tom Sawyer*.

"You got to go all by yourself, to the middle of the woods, where you know there's a spunk-water stump, a rotten stump where the rain water was. Just as it's midnight you back up against the stump and jam your hand in and say: 'Barley-corn, barley corn, injun-meal shorts, spunk water, spunk water, swaller these warts,' and then walk away quick, eleven steps, with your eyes shut and then turn around three times and walk home without speaking to anybody. Because if you speak the charm's busted...

"Sometimes I take 'em off with a bean. You take and split the bean, and cut the wart so as to get some blood, and then you put the blood on one piece of the bean and take and dig a hole and bury it 'bout midnight at the crossroads in the dark of the moon, and then you burn up the rest of the bean. You see that piece that's got the blood on it will keep drawing and drawing, trying to fetch the other piece to it, and so that helps the blood to draw the wart, and pretty soon off she comes. Though when you're burying it, if you say 'Down bean; off, wart; come no more to bother me!' It's better."

"I believe that if I ever had to practice cannibalism, I might manage if there was enough tarragon around." James Beard

Dog

Joseph Conrad (1857-1924) was born in Poland and did not learn English until he was in his twenties. His politically oriented father died young but not before he wrote poems, plays and translated Shakespeare. Joseph went to sea and for some 20 years, made his life as a sailor and wrote his first work at the age of 36. He gave up the sea in 1894 and turned his life toward writing.

He married two years later, had two sons, and wrote the introduction for a cookbook his wife wrote. Jessie Conrad wrote *A Handbook of Cookery for a Small House* in 1923. Joseph wrote in the introduction, "Such undertakings are above suspicion for their object can conceivably be no other than to increase the happiness of mankind."

Conrad wrote with great depth and some of his best works are *Heart of Darkness, Typhoon, Lord Jim, Nostromo,* and many others. In a short work something like an autobiography, entitled *Personal Record,* he wrote about soldiers in Napoleon's Army who were reduced to eating a dog to survive. Conrad's reactions were like many who felt that eating a dog was as abominable as eating a person.

"Late in the night the rash counsels of hunger overcame the dictates of prudence...A dog barked and dashed out through a gap in the fence... His head, I understand, was severed at one blow from his body. They had not killed the dog for the sake of his pelt. He was large. He was eaten. The rest is silence. A silence in which a small boy shudders and says firmly, 'I could not have eaten that dog.'

"And his grandmother remarks with a smile, 'Perhaps you don't know what it is to be hungry.'"

"Chorizos are made for as many days as there are in a year, that is to say 365 chorizos and another 50 for the days when there are guests." Alexander Dumas (1802-1870) on Spanish cuisine.

Duck Gravy

Ernest Hemingway (1899-1961) wrote *Death in the Afternoon* in 1932. He had an interesting variation on Duck Gravy.

"In front of the barn a woman held a duck whose throat she had cut and stroked him gently while a little girl held a cup to catch the blood for making gravy. The duck seemed very contented and when they put him down (the blood all in the cup) he waddled twice and found that he was dead. We ate him later, stuffed and roasted; and many other dishes, with the wine of that year and the year before and the great year four years before that and other years that I lost track of."

"Once in the wilds of Afghanistan, I lost my corkscrew, and we were forced to live on nothing but food and water for days." W. C. Fields (1879-1946)

Eggs

James Thurber (1894-1961) wrote, in *Thurber Country,* about a man who didn't know how to cook but after several hours without his wife's presence, entered the kitchen.

"He realizes that he should probably find the refrigerator, which he finally does, peering helplessly inside, getting his forefinger stuck into something cold and sticky, and, at length, removing a head of lettuce wrapped in cheesecloth and two eggs. He sets these on the kitchen table, but the eggs begin to roll, so he puts them in his pocket. He remembers Christopher Columbus's solution of the problem of how to keep an egg from rolling. He takes out one of the eggs, strikes one end of it smartly on top of the table, and produces a small pool of yolk and white. The egg does not stand on end as it should. It leaks.

"The project of cooking something is completely abandoned, for he is faced with a much more urgent task: how to get rid of the mess he has created with the egg, and prevent his wife from finding out about it when she comes home. He tries to pick up the spattered egg, with no success. So he looks around for a cloth, and spots one neatly folded over the back of a kitchen chair. On this, he wipes his eggy hands and, as the cloth falls open, he sees that what he has hold of is an apron. Panic seizes him now, and he wipes up the broken egg with the apron. This doesn't seem to work too well, so he gets water in a glass and pours it on the tabletop and then wipes some more.

"The dilemma now is what to do with the apron. Many a husband, living in the country, would get the spade and bury the apron outdoors, but John is at heart a city man. He stuffs the apron in the wastebasket, but even as he does so, the dreadful compulsion is forming at the back of his mind to wash out the evidence of his guilt. He takes the apron from the wastebasket, runs a tub of hot water, and douses the apron. What he has now is something so wet that it cannot possibly be dried before his wife gets home. Every husband must work out this quandary in his own way."

"Against the disease of writing one must take special precautions, since it is a dangerous and contagious disease." Pierre Abelard (1079-1142)

Entrance to a Cafe

Edgar Allen Poe (1809-1849) wrote a beautiful description about the entrance to the café of a great chef named Bon-Bon in his short story entitled *"Bon-Bon."*

"To enter the little café in the cul-de-sac Le Febre was, at the period of our tale, to enter the sanctum of a man of genius. Bon-Bon was a man of genius. There was not a sous-cuisinier in Rouen who could not have told you that Bon-Bon was a man of genius. His very cat knew it, and forebore to whisk her tail in the presence of the man of genius. His large water-dog was acquainted with the fact, and upon the approach of his master, betrayed his sense of inferiority by a sanctity of deportment, a debasement of the ears, and a dropping of the lower jaw not altogether unworthy of a dog."

"What's drinking? A mere pause from thinking!" George Gordon, Lord Byron (1788-1824)

Hangover Cures

Romans used to eat boiled cabbage before retiring after drinking heavily, to carry alcohol out of the body.

Antiphanes (388-311 B.C.) was the first to mention using a "hair of the dog that bit you" to cure a hangover.

The Scots used to drink Irn Bru (pronounced Iron Brew) which con-sisted of a glass of water with sugar dissolved in it. They also drank sweet cups of tea.

Alistair Maclean (1922-1987) Scottish writer of *The Guns of Navarone* and *HMS Ulysses* believed he got relief from a breakfast of kippers mari-nated in lemon juice.

Robert Benchley (1889-1945), humorist and writer, said, "There is no cure for a hangover save death."

Wine writer Andre Simon thought raw herring served with onions and sour cream were of help the next morning.

Ernest Hemingway wrote *A Farewell to Arms* in 1929. He had an inter-esting antidote for drunkenness.

"You better not go up there drunk."

"I'm not drunk, Rinin. Really."

"You'd better chew some coffee."

"Nonsense."

"I'll get some, baby. You walk up and down." He came back with a handful of roasted coffee beans. "Chew those, baby, and God be with you."

"Curlylocks, Curlylocks, wilt thou be mine?
Thou shalt not wash dishes nor yet feed the swine,
But sit on a cushion and sew a fine seam,
And feed upon strawberries, sugar and cream."
Anonymous

Honeymoon Strawberries

Diane Holloway was a psychologist and "Drug Czar" of Dallas, Texas. She co-authored *Before You Say 'I Quit'* with Nancy Bishop, and wrote *The*

Mind of Oswald and *Analyzing Leaders, Presidents and Terrorists*. She co-authored *Dallas and the Jack Ruby Trial* and *American History in Song* with Bob Cheney. She organized the Sun Cities Authors' Association in the West Valley of Phoenix, Arizona.

Diane married Bob Cheney in 1980. They honeymooned in Mexico City. Awaiting them in their room were fresh luscious strawberries, brown sugar, sour cream, and a bottle of champagne. The simple combination of strawberries dipped in sour cream and brown sugar was so special that Bob and Diane continue to celebrate their anniversary with that treat.

"The two Christians met on the way many people who were going to their towns, women and men, with a firebrand (cigar) in the hand, and herbs to drink and smoke thereof, as they are accustomed." Christopher Columbus (1451-1506) 1492 upon discovering America

Pemican from Longfellow

Pemican is a sort of jerky that was easy to carry when traveling. The Indians made several versions and one served at Hiawatha's wedding feast was described by Henry Wadsworth Longfellow (1807-1882) in *The Song of Hiawatha*.

"First they ate the sturgeon, Nahma,
And the pike, the Maskenoxha,
Caught and cooked by old Nokomis;
Then on pemican they feasted,
Pemican and buffalo marrow,
Haunch of deer and hump of bison,
Yellow cakes of the Mondamin,
And the wild rice of the river."

"If you are a rich man, whenever you please; and if you are a poor man, whenever you can." Diogenes (around 320 B.C.) reply when asked what was the proper time for supper

Pemican from Ogalala Sioux

This version of pemican or jerky was made with deer. It called for flavorful additions which made it more palatable. The Indians carried this ready source of meat about with them to tide them over between periods of famine.

"Put clean dried meat in a bread pan and roast. When ready, sprinkle some water on the roasted meat. Then cool and wrap meat in a clean white cloth. Pound until the meat is very tender and flaky. Add tallow grease, sugar and raisins to taste."

"Pease porridge hot, pease porridge cold,
Pease porridge in the pot, nine days old."
Anonymous

Scottish Porridge

Oatmeal was considered "the backbone of many a sturdy Scotsman." Porridge was one of the main ways of eating oats, in days gone by. It is important to obtain good quality medium-ground oats (rather than rolled oats) and to keep stirring it to avoid solid lumps. This recipe is available on the Internet.

- 2 cups water (or 1 cup water, 1 cup milk)
- 2 ½ rounded tablespoons medium-ground oats
- Pinch of salt

Bring the water (or water and milk) to a good rolling boil, preferably in a non-stick pan. Slowly pour the oatmeal into the boiling liquid, stirring vigorously all the time. Keep stirring until it has returned to the boil again, reduce the heat, cover the pan and simmer very gently for 15 minutes, stirring frequently. Add the salt at this point and simmer and stir for a further 5-10 minutes. It should be thick but pourable.

Traditions:
1. Stir the porridge clockwise
2. Porridge is eaten standing up (either out of respect for the noble dish or because busy farmers are doing other things while eating it.)
3. Some frown on sugar in porridge but others approve or suggest a "tot" of whiskey. (See the recipe for Atholl Brose.)
4. Porridge used to be served with separate bowls of double cream. A spoonful of porridge was dipped into a communal bowl of cream before eating.
5. Porridge used to be poured into a "porridge drawer" and, once it had cooled, could be cut up into slices. These were easier to carry than brittle oatcakes.

"Chacun a son gout" or *"Each to his own taste."* From *Die Fledermaus* by Carl Haffner, Richard Genee and Johann Strauss

Termite Food

Humorous poet Ogden Nash (1902-1971) wrote a darling poem about the food of even the lowly termite.

"Some primal termite knocked on wood
And tasted it, and found it good,
And that is why your Cousin May
Fell through the parlor floor today."

"But I don't want nutrition. I want food!" Alice B. Toklas (1877-1967)

Water

Samuel Taylor Coleridge (1772-1834) wrote *The Rime of the Ancient Mariner.* Despite the fact that the ship was sailing amidst water, it was undrinkable saltwater and the sailors were dying.

"Water, water every where,
And all the boards did shrink;
Water, water, everywhere
Nor any drop to drink."

"My doctor told me to stop having intimate dinners for four. Unless there are three other people." Orson Welles (1915-1985)

Zombie

Zora Neale Hurston (1891-1960) was an American author who wrote stories and anthropological folklore. She said, "The force from somewhere in Space which commands you to write in the first place, gives you no choice. You take up the pen when you are told, and write what is commanded. There is no agony like bearing an untold story inside you." She wrote this recipe in *Tell My Horse* which came from a phrase used in Voodoo ceremonies where the person becomes possessed by a spirit and is ridden like a horse by the spirit.

- One Puffer fish
- One dose scopalomine
- One dose atropine

First, you must become a Haitian Voodoo Witch Doctor, called a Bokor, which can be attained by distance learning without the need of attending a university. Zora studied under famous anthropologist Frank Boas and went to Haiti and Jamaica to learn about Bokors.

Then blend a puffer fish into a tasty dish and feed it to a potential zombie, perhaps a couch potato. The fish has a poison called tetrodotoxin, which is a potent ion channel blocker. It can kill but at other times just lowers the metabolism so that the person is thought to be dead. But don't bury them. It's hard to live beneath six feet of earth. Just put the body someplace out of the way.

When you are ready to bring them back to life and have them roaming your streets, make a paste containing atropine and scopalomine and whatever else you have in the kitchen. These are hallucinogens. The victim was first "killed" and now brought back to life walking the earth.

Get in the mood watching *White Zombie* of 1932 with Bela Lugosi or *The Walking Dead* of 1936 with Boris Karloff and Edmund Gwenn or *Night of the Living Dead*, the 1968 thriller. If they don't work, *Zombies of the Stratosphere*, 1958, with Leonard Nimoy will make you a Zombie and you'll walk right out of the room in a daze.

For the Zombie drink, here's a great recipe:
- 3 ounces dark rum
- 1 ounce light rum
- 1 ounce lime juice
- 1 ounce pineapple juice
- 1 ounce orange juice
- 2 teaspoons sugar
- 2 teaspoons 151 proof rum
- 2 orange slices
- 2 maraschino cherries
- 2 mint sprigs

Chill 2 highball glasses, combine all ingredients in a blender except the 151 proof rum, orange slices, cherries and mint. Blend 30 seconds on high. Pour into glass, float 1 teaspoon 151 proof rum in each drink. Garnish with orange slice, cherry and mint sprig. Only one will make you walk like a zombie. Serves 2.

SOURCES AND REFERENCES

Allen, Stewart Lee. *In the Devil's Garden*. New York: Ballentine Books, 2002.

Ambrose, Stephen. *Undaunted Courage*. New York: Simon & Schuster, 1996.

Apron Strings. Little Rock: Junior League of Little Rock, 1997.

Auel, Jean. *The Clan of the Cave Bear*. New York: Crown Publishers, 1980.

Barry, Dave. *Dave Barry Turns 50*. New York: Crown Publishers, 1998.

Bombeck, Erma. *Forever, Erma*. Kansas City: Andrews and McMeel, 1996.

Bombeck, Erma. *Family: The Ties That Bind...and Gag*. New York: McGraw-Hill Book Co., 1987.

Boreth, Craig. *The Hemingway Cookbook*. Chicago: Chicago Review Press, 1998.

Chandler, Raymond. *The Long Goodbye*. New York: Vintage Crime/Black Lizard, 1953.

Claiborne, Craig. *The New New York Times Cookbook*. New York: Wings Book, 1975.

Conrad, Barnaby. *The Martini*. New York: Chronicle Books, 1995.

Cowley, Malcolm Ed. *Hemingway*. New York: The Viking Press, 1944.

Desert Caballeros Western Museum. *Dude Food and Ranch Stories*. Wickenburg, Arizona, 1999.

Hammett, Dashiell. *The Big Knockover and Selected Short Stories*. New York: Vintage Books, 1972.

Hemingway, Ernest. *A Farewell to Arms.* New York: Charles Scribner's Sons, 1929.

Hillman, James & Boer, Charles, Ed. *Freud's Own Cookbook.* New York: Harper Row Publishers, 1985.

Horowitz, Paul, Ed. *Collected Stories of O. Henry.* New York: Avenel Books, 1986.

Hurston, Zora Neale. *Tell My Horse.* New York: HarperColliers, 1937.

Karon, Jan. *A Common Life: The Wedding Story.* New York: Viking, 2001.

Keillor, Garrison. *Leaving Home.* New York: Viking Press, 1987.

Ketcham, Richard. *Will Rogers: His Life and Times.* New York: American Heritage Publishing Co., 1973.

Longfellow, Henry. *The Song of Hiawatha.* Boston: Tickner & Fields, originally 1856.

Marshall, Brenda. *The Charles Dickens Cookbook.* Toronto: Personal Library, 1981.

McCrone, Carol and Rose-Hancock, Margaret, Ed. *Fresh, Fast and Fabulous Cookbook.* Seattle: Psychoanalytic Association of Seattle, 1982.

Melville, Herman. *Moby Dick.* New York: Penguin, New York, 2001 (originally 1851).

Newman, Paul and Hotchner, A. E. *Newman's Own Cookbook.* New York: Simon & Schuster, 1998.

Poe, Edgar Allen. *The Complete Tales and Poems of Edgar Allen Poe.* New York: Vintage Books, 1975.

Price, Mary and Vincent. *A Treasury of Great Recipes.* New York: Grosset & Dunlap, 1965.

Price, Victoria. *Vincent Price.* New York: St. Martin's Press, 1999.

Reichl, Ruth. *Comfort Me With Apples.* Waterville, Maine: G. K. Hall & Co., 2001.

Sanders, Lawrence. *The Third Deadly Sin.* New York: G. P. Putnam's Sons, 1981.

Santayana, George. *Persons and Places: The Background of My Life.* New York: Scribner, 1944.

Steinbeck, John. *Cannery Row.* New York: The Viking Press, 1945.

Stout, Rex. *The Nero Wolfe Cookbook.* New York: The Viking Press, 1973.

Thackeray, William. "The Ballad of Bouillabaisse," *Blackwood's Magazine.* Jan., 1854.

Thurber, James. *Thurber Country.* New York: Simon and Schuster, 1953.

Toklas, Alice. *The Alice B. Toklas Cook Book.* New York: Harper Collins, 1986.

Twain, Mark. *The Adventures of Tom Sawyer.* New York: Readers Digest, 1932 (originally 1876).

Van Doren, Carl, Ed. *The Borzoi Reader.* New York: Alfred Knopf, 1936.

Voltaire, Francois. *Candide.* New York: Concord Books, 1930 (originally 1759).

Sun Cities Authors Association

Our thanks go to the members of the Sun Cities Authors Association for their mutual support of each other and for their many literary projects. The members are:

Susan Alander, Bev Allen, Gerrie Anderson, Ruthmarie Arguello-Sheehan, Lillian Asbell, Mike Basford, Lucy Bee, Gerry Benninger, Eileen Birin, Lydia Boyer, Cecile Brandon, Bob Brisson, Joyce Brown, Gene Carara, Adrienne Carpenter, Louis Cavagnaro, Bob Cheney, Harold Coffman, Don Connors, Gordon Crandall, Nancy Damato, Nancy Dammann, Dr. Ralph Daniel, George Davis, Mike Dubin, John Findley, Maita Floyd, Robert Frieders, Lois Gentry, Dr. Richard Girard, Cy Greenhalgh, Anita Hamilton, Flo Heine, Virginia Holen, Dr. Diane Holloway, Dr. Angela Holman, Hazel Jaworski, Claudette Jeffrey, Evelyn King, John Larson, Robert Laumeyer, Dorothy Crane Lazzerini, Frederick Lenhart, Beverly Littlejohn, Cleo Lorette, J. Angus MacDonald, Greta Manville, Kay Meier, Rabbi Seymour Moskowitz, Eleanor Nelson, Dr. Max Oppenheimer, Phyllis Orsi, Esther Paige, Peggy Parsons, Thelma Patrick, Lizlee Payant, Beverly Petrone, Dr. Bob Quinn, Dr. Dan Rice, Harold Richman, Anne Schaetzel, Eleanor Schneider, Patricia Scott, Lee Shaffer, Thayer Soule, Penina Keen Spinka, Betty Baker Spohr, Johannes Spreen, Fawn Stitman, Betty Stoneking, Bill Svoboda, Barbara Talacek, Louis Venditti, Dr. Daniel Wagner, Harry Warren, Patti Warren, William R. Webb, Nora Wellnitz, Lamont Wharton, George Williams, Ann Helen Winsor,

The home office is Sun Cities Authors Association, 20402 N. 150th Dr., Sun City West, Arizona 85375.

About the Author

The editor, Dr. Diane Holloway, was a Dallas psychologist and ultimately the "Drug Czar" of Dallas until the end of the 1980s. She retired and moved to Sun City West, Arizona, where she has organized the Sun Cities Authors Association and has written several books. She co-authored *Before You Say 'I Quit'* with Nancy Bishop, she co-authored *Dallas and the Jack Ruby Trial* and *American History in Song* with historian Bob Cheney. She wrote *The Mind of Oswald, Bon Appetit,* and *Analyzing Leaders, Presidents and Terrorists.*

Before she began her professional training and life, she followed in the footsteps of literary figures by living in London and Paris in the late 1950s, hanging out in the same cafes and sites as those figures described in this book. She has always had an affection for writers, the written word, as well as for all those who struggle to fulfill themselves emotionally and artistically. For that reason, she has tried to assist the budding talents of those who decided to write in later life.

Index